Virtute et claritate

O' Hara

ISBN-13: 978-0615534459

ISBN-10: 0615534457

THE INFERNUS FILES
BY
PATRICK SEAMUS O'HARA

This book is dedicated to all my friends at Steve Ray's Catholic Convert forum who, through constant encouragement and sometimes scolding, have molded me in to the Catholic I am today.

PREFACE

It is not known exactly how these messages came to be lodged in the in box of the computer residing in the offices of Father Daniel Baker of St. Mary the Immaculate parish. The first of these messages was considered by Father Baker to be an elongated prank, and regretfully, was permanently deleted from his inbox. In retrospect we wish we could have that one to study also. The information which has been gleaned from these messages has been passed on to the Vatican for further review.

The second message was also considered a prank, but after reading the subject matter, and finding the missive interesting, even as a joke, Father Baker decided to keep it. As you will see by the nature of the instruction contained in the Email, there is a whole genre of lessons being taught about which we in the Church have neglected to warn our converts.

Upon further consideration, Father Baker called in Bishop Creen to look with him at the unusual subject matter within the correspondence. Providentially, it was at the very time that Bishop Creen was reading this first saved missive, annotated here as Chapter One, that another Email popped up in Fr. Baker's inbox. While there was still the sense that this could be nothing more than a prank, the tone and tenor of the writing of the first two missives seemed too well crafted to be that of a prankster. It was just a little too theologically literate. Most pranksters are not all that intelligent and their efforts are both mundane and pedestrian at best. Sort of like those "phishing" letters from the supposed wives of deposed African kings who are looking for help in protecting their millions.

We have since determined that these Emails are quite authentic. What convinced us of this was the incredible discovery that these events took place right here in our quiet little parish town. How this portal to the unseen world happened to open we do not know, other than to attribute this to the provident hand of the all wise God. We have been given important information. It remains to be seen what shall come of it.

It is my hope that the Church will seriously consider publication of these messages, inasmuch as they give to us a valuable insight into the spiritual realm and the devious thinking which goes into destroying our Lord's Church. While we do know that ultimately our Lord will reign victorious, do we not have a great responsibility to cooperate with God's grace and warn as many people as we can about the many traps that Satan places in the path of the believer? Even more so, judging from the content of these Emails, is the importance of understanding why it is so hard to attract converts to the Faith and what they face when they begin their initial investigation of the Faith. It is the sworn desire of our nemesis, the Evil One of old, to keep the Church from being one again and to keep the state of dissension among us at a fever pitch. A united Church would be a formidable foe, therefore, every convert who comes into our Lord's Church is one step closer to our bringing a powerful grace to bear on evil which would be their ruin in this world.

Since Fr. Baker has shared these with me as my pastor and spiritual director, I hope you will feel free to share them with your friends in the Church. It is our hope that by whatever means possible, Catholics will be brought to read this correspondence and once again come to realize the seriousness of the battle in which we are engaged as members of our Lord's Church.

CHAPTER ONE

From: darktormentum@ lake_of_fire. org

To: grasshopper@ tormentmasters. com

Nephew Glimslug –

WHAT! is this rumor which comes to me regarding you and your subject? You have been given one subject as the merest of apprentice demons, and it comes to my ears that you somehow cannot even keep him from reading the writings of the Early Fathers! How could you think to allow him near that horrid bunch of misfits who turned the world upside down for the Enemy? Is there not enough of vapid and brain dead TV programs to distract his attention sufficiently? Is there not enough of sports games, movies, and Internet – that particularly wonderful invention which our Master, in his infernal wisdom, hijacked and turned into a moveable feast of pornography on demand – to prevent this from happening? Listen, I know your subject loves baseball and his team has prospects of a very good season ahead of them. Are you telling me that you can't even get him interested in wasting his time on drafting a fantasy team for this coming year? What is wrong with you? These are the most easily distracted of creatures, and you need to be about putting him in a distracted state. This nasty little turn of events poses a serious danger to our plans for his ultimate destruction and eternal damnation!

Do you have any idea *at all* of the spiritual dynamite that your subject is playing with? Just for your information, let me give you a few quotes (if I can do so without losing my lunch all over my desk):

"Our sin will not be small if we eject from the episcopate those who blamelessly and holily have offered its Sacrifices. (St. Clement, bishop of Rome – 80 A.D. Letter to the Corinthians)

His assembly teaches him that the Mass is no sacrifice, that this was an invention of the Council of Trent, and yet here is one of the first Church leaders in the Christian faith teaching that indeed they do offer Sacrifice. This quote, should he discover it, is guaranteed to get him thinking and wondering why his assembly doesn't believe that it is a Sacrifice. There is a reason we have worked so hard to keep these disciples of the Apostles unknown to both the average Protestant and

Catholic. We don't want your subject even remotely thinking that the first Christians held distinctly Catholic beliefs. And we certainly don't wish the pew slugs in the Catholic Church to realize what they have their hands upon.

"Consider how contrary to the mind of God are the heterodox in regard to the grace of God which has come to us. They have no regard for charity, none for the widow, the orphan, the oppressed, none for the man in prison, the hungry or the thirsty. They abstain from the Eucharist and from prayer, because they do not admit that the Eucharist is the flesh of our Savior Jesus Christ, the flesh which suffered for our sins and which the Father, in His graciousness, raised from the dead." (St. Ignatius of Antioch –"Letter to the Smyrnaeans," paragraph 6. circa 80-110 A.D.)

He fellowships with people who do not admit that the Eucharist is the flesh of the Enemy. Do you really want him reading this and asking himself the kind of questions that this will raise in his mind? He thinks that his Presbyterian Calvinism is Christian orthodoxy of the highest and best kind. Do you really want him discovering that what the Early Fathers taught totally contradicts what his assembly teaches and that the Early Fathers would consider him and such beliefs to be heretical? Have you lost your mind?

Ugh. One more. Just one.

4

"I have not taste for the food that perishes nor for the pleasures of this life. I want the Bread of God which is the Flesh of Christ, who was the seed of David: and for drink I desire His Blood which is love that cannot be destroyed." (St. Ignatius of Antioch – Letter to the Romans paragraph 7, circa 80-110 A.D.)

Disgusting! That is *quite* enough. As it is I am going to be sick at my stomach for a week for having have convey this nauseating filth to you. I hope you and your mother appreciate the disgusting lengths to which I am going to in order to instruct and form you into a demon worthy of serving our infernal Master! All your subject has to do is to read a collection of such quotes and he will begin to realize that the comfy little assembly in which he is safely ensconced in no way can be found in the writings of the earliest Christian leaders. The great majority of today's deluded Christians actually think that their chosen form of worship is what they call "New Testament worship." They like to think that they have what they fondly refer to as a "New Testament church." But when they find the writings of the very first Christians – these disgusting Early Fathers I just quoted to you – they began to realize they have been considerably led astray in doctrine by their leaders.

Then the real trouble will begin, for I have observed your subject and I know his type. He is disgustingly inquisitive. Instead of settling quietly in his pew and minding his own theological business like the great majority of lazy and ignorant human beings – oh, no! – this one you have been assigned to is a reader, a student, dreadfully curious, and always asking questions. Just the kind that we hate! It is, in a way, almost unfair that your very first subject is of such a mind, but it is what it is, and you simply are going to have to deal with it.

But worse than that, how could you possibly have been so derelict as to allow him a chance meeting with that pestilent convert to the Catholic Faith, M. Jenkins? Jenkins is a walking, talking encyclopedia of those Early Fathers, the bane of the underworld, and every demon worth the fires of hell steers his subjects on a wide path away from this turncoat who escaped our clutches. You should have been on high alert the minute your subject asked a question about St. Irenaeus in his Sunday School. If you had been so alert, you would have known to have set a wide path for him away from Jenkins, and we would not have this problem on our hands. Instead, because of your dereliction of duty, your subject now comes away from this chance meeting pondering and thinking, and you know how we hate to have any of these foolish creatures thinking.

A Catholic, even with the slightest bit of knowledge, is bad enough itself, but a convert doubly so, for they are not only absolutely filled with every knowledge of Catholic doctrine imaginable, having studied their way into the enemy's Church, but they are absolutely overflowing with zeal. Disgusting zeal! They actually believe that everyone should be Catholic like they are. They have the nerve to go to family, friends, and especially former religious associates and actually try to open their eyes to the truths that we have so well obscured for the last five centuries, beginning with our faithful servants, Calvin and Luther.

Speaking of whom, I understand that the nasty French lawyer and that fat little German monk continue a most gratifying howling and screaming in Purgatory. They are both lucky indeed that our Enemy is of such a forgiving character that He even forgives those who turn against Him if they will show but the slightest repentance. Our Enemy is entirely too kind to those who oppose Him.

Stupid rebels! Luther was such an emotional train wreck that it was almost too easy to convince him that God hated him. But Calvin. Now there was a bit of a challenge, and a very enjoyable one at that. It was especially such fun to take his vaunted intellect and twist his theological training with a fine vintage of Rationalism. Using his own powers of intellect, I turned him in rebellion against the Church of the Enemy and the truth contained therein. Now with every soul that falls into our clutches from a non-Catholic assembly, his torment is increased exponentially, even though he is only in Purgatory. Ah, what a marvelous price sin demands! It is quite enjoyable to drop by Purgatory and listen for a while to the agony he is going through as all that rebellion and self-will is purged from him. He was a great servant to us, and I <u>hate him</u> – with every fiber of my being!

Yes, I was there when he was on his deathbed and it was

absolutely delicious to see the look of utter horror and amazement on his face when he realized what he had done and what he was facing for his arrogance and rebellion against that authority which our Enemy has invested in that motley collection mere human beings called the Church. He expected a direct express to Heaven due to that wonderful doctrine of election we gave to him. And the most utterly perfect irony of it all is that he always thought of himself as being such a wonderful servant of our hated Enemy! Ah, if only he had not mustered that one last cry for mercy!

"Faith alone" is a guarantee of Heaven," he said. *"Works aren't at all necessary for eternal life."* One wonders what parts of our Enemy's accursed Book this chap was reading? It certainly wasn't John 5: 28-29 or Romans 2: 5-10. He certainly missed large sections of the Epistle of James also.

For all his intellect, which I will admit to be a tad more than the average slug in the pew, for all of his high sounding writings, his overabundant use of the most impressive sounding words, his appeals to Greek and Hebrew, his long, windy sermons that seemed like they would never end, he still somehow entirely missed whole sections of the Enemy's Book that warn these creatures that they must be about good works and they are going to be judged on the quality of those works.

Amazing! How easy it was to puff a little pride into his ear and get him to believe himself to be the apex of intellectual thought and theological learning. What a bubbling cauldron of insanity that he, a mere insect with neither apostolic authority nor promise of infallibility, would position himself against the Enemy's Church and the charism of infallibility and authority the Enemy gave to it!

What pathetic little fools these creatures are, so braggadocios in their ignorance of spiritual truths. From Arius, to Sabellius, right up to Luther and Calvin, and then the thousands we have at this very time, how easy they have been to trick. No wonder the Enemy's book says that pride goes before a fall. All a demon ever has to do is to convince one of these creatures that he is by far the brightest of all in his assembly, and he will take that intellectual pride and set himself up as the final authority on all matters spiritual. It almost takes all the fun out of our work of opposing the Church and destroying souls.

How I love hearing ignoramuses thump their Bibles, foaming at the mouth, while they scream "The Word of God says this, and the Word of God says that." All the while, they really don't have a _clue_ as to what they are talking about. It is just too good.

This is why pride is the first deadly sin, to which all others are inferior. You must observe closely and learn well how it blinds men to the truth. This is your lesson for this week. When you are finished with this Email, I want you to go to the Academy's library and check out Volume III of DECEITS OF THE REFORMATION, by our esteemed Professor Slimeous. There is much valuable information, with charts and pictures, showing not only how we used such pride and vainglory to start the Protestant Rebellion, but how it has been kept well alive over the centuries through the same pride. Pride is the foundation of all that we achieve against our Enemy's Kingdom, and without it, we would have little toe hold with these miserable creatures. Humility is by far the worst thing that can happen to one of your subjects. It is the door which opens these hairless apes to salvation and a real relationship to our Enemy, and thus we hate to see it develop in our subjects.

I shall give you a little lesson now on how to use pride in our work. When one of the Enemy's agents engages one of our subjects and gives that subject a taste of His truth regarding the Church, the first thing you must place in the mind of the subject is the thought, *"Why, surely "I" couldn't be wrong!"* Then you must follow this up with a list of certain books to study– books written by our agents on earth. We have a delightful earthly collection of mistranslations of the Enemy's Book, along with twisted and distorted commentaries which we have inspired for centuries from the pens of men who had no more knowledge of truth than an ant has of what causes rain.

Imagine your subject trying to find the truth by studying the writings of someone who is just as confused, disoriented, and deceived as he is. And all the time your subject thinks these writings to be from a superior intellect and worthy of study. My nephew, that is just tooooooo charming to watch! You will come to absolutely love such displays of ignorance on their part and the resulting arrogance it breeds in them.

For instance, listening to certain Anabaptists among the humans earnestly declare that the KJV1611AVis the text from which Jesus preached. I know you are laughing on the other side of your screen, but I kid you not! I will find and send you the website later.

This study can be most profitable to you if you apply yourself to it. Use your current subject for practice and get him away from those Early Fathers! I want you on this – *immediately!*

Aggrandize the authors of our rebellion in his mind. Encourage your subject to think that men such as Calvin, Hodges, Edwards, Boettner, and the whole host of those miserable rebels, are almost godlike in their brilliance and theological learning. Then be sure to place in his mind continued thoughts that Catholic apologists, even the Early Fathers who learned from the Apostles themselves, are at best semi-literate morons who couldn't hold a candle to a Reformed theologian. Remember this phrase: "*After all, people in those days were unlearned."* Season your subject's mind carefully with that great flavoring!

After that is done, take one theme, such as why the Eucharist couldn't possibly be the true Body and Blood of the Enemy, and bring to your subject's attention all the writings by those in our camp who defend this position.

Now, in the future, whenever you use this tactic make sure you properly tailor the writings to the intellect of your subject. The mundane and pedestrian writings of Oliver B. Greene will be of scant interest to a Covenant Dominion Theologian of Calvinist bent. Likewise, those in the AOG are not really interested in what John Calvin had to say. Feed them a steady diet of Jimmy Swaggart's delusions.

Go now. And may Darkness be with you as you begin your career for our dark and eternal Master.

In service to his Eternal Darkness, I remain,

Your Master and Uncle, Infernus.

CHAPTER TWO

From: darktormentum @ lake_of_fire.org

To: grasshopper @ tormentmasters.com

Trainee Glimslug!

I hope for your sake you have had a profitable week and your lesson books are well in order since my last Email. I do not take well to trainees goofing off when they should have been studying – and I have some disturbing reports on your behavior! Let me remind you that I am a master of painful discipline, and if I find these reports to be true, you shall learn the hard way just how little I care for our relationship as uncle and nephew. Remember your place and apply yourself! Your carefree days as an imp are over!

Now let us return to the issue of your subject. I am greatly concerned as I observe him, and it has been only with great difficulty that I have intervened to slow him down a notch while you were studying (or playing around with your imp buddies, as the case may be). He is becoming a danger to us and to the territory. We do not want another M. Jenkins on our hands. One is quite enough in any territory, and your territory has become very unstable as of late. You can mark this down as truth from hell: converts are worse than lice! Put one in a town and leave him unmolested by our servants, and in six months you will have twenty just like him! In a couple of years you could be looking at a whole new parish for the Enemy, complete with numerous programs to advance the Enemy's kingdom. Terrible! And we have been suffering far, far too many losses lately.

Do you remember that Scott Hahn fiasco? Do I really have to drag out that whole unsavory mess and go over it again with you? We had that boy in the palm of our hot little hands and your stupid cousin Frumdung couldn't keep him distracted well enough (for which he is paying dearly in shrieking torment even as I write this) to keep him from leaving our camp. And now, to make matters worse, not only has Hahn helped thousands to defect to the Enemy's camp – he *teaches*! Yes, he actually teaches those abominable truths that we hate. He has made scores of baby-faced warriors in clerical collars that we now must contend with. And all this as we thought our Master was on the verge of closing down that entire dreadful Church of our Enemy once and for all due to lack of vocations.

We were so close! The Enemy's seminaries were practically empty, and those that were filled were filled with unbelievers who were a great asset in the latest Church scandal. The monasteries were almost void of those disgusting prayer warriors called monks, and this whole generation simply laughed at the idea of following the Enemy into such a repressive life. But look now! A trickle of interest began with this Scott Hahn, and other converts like him who proclaim the Enemy's message with clarity and boldness, and as a result, we see these empty buildings slowly filling up again, and this time, with men who are orthodox and determined to be holy and serve our Enemy with all their being!

What did you say? Silence them?

Did I actually hear you suggest the use of violence against them? Come, nephew! Were you not required to pass History of Martyrs 101 before you came to me? Is old Dumfrumas letting you novices reach graduation now by grading on a curve? You should know that there is no silencing this bunch. Even their deaths speak loudly, and make scores of converts to their cause. This is why it is so important to _neutralize_ their message.

No, unfortunately, we will never be able to destroy the truth, but if there is no one to proclaim it and administer it in the sacraments to their faithful, then who cares how much they know? The idea that eternal life is somehow found in holding properly to a set of ideas in a certain fashion is the cornerstone of the Reformation. *"Faith alone,"* remember? In our assemblies, it's what you know of the Enemy's book – not how you treat your fellow man.

Of course, that isn't what the Enemy taught them when He walked among them. He told them that eternal life was to be found in the Sacrament of eating His Flesh and drinking His Blood. In other words, it is through the sacramental life that a sinner enters into and maintains eternal life. The Eucharist brings the Enemy right into their very beings, and gives them not only life, but a real hope of being with the Enemy forever, and we do not wish that at all. Truth without Sacraments is like an automobile without gasoline. Totally worthless. Therefore, we must continue to attempt the destruction of the Enemy's seminaries, and at all costs to discourage these vermin from taking vows. We don't care what they actually know in their puny ant minds, we just don't want them to be able to get valid Sacraments from validly ordained priests.

You have no idea how many Protestants – absolutely filled with book knowledge and seminary degrees – we have reaped for our Master. Their arrogant denial of the Eucharist is the best thing we have going for us. What great pains they take to write long and wordy sermons which heap scorn upon the very thing that would save their miserable souls. Scott Hahn is beyond a nuisance. He and others like him are destructive of everything we have worked so hard to build, and we can ill afford your subject to become another like unto him, and especially in your territory, being what it is.

Yes, I know we have a number of fifth columnists within the Enemy's Church, and they area great source of pride and consolation to our dreadful Master. From bishops down to mere laity, they oppose the very Church to which they are supposed to be faithful, teaching our lovely ideas of abortion rights, women's ordination, and so-called gay "marriage." You can study how this came to pass in Goatamus' book LIBERALIZING THE ENEMY'S TRUTH -Vol. 2. Add it to your list of required reading, and have it finished by the end of next week! The infiltration of these wonderfully vile concepts was a long and arduous process, but it is reaping great rewards for us now as it comes into full fruit.

One of my greatest enjoyments from this work is those marvelous New Age mantras chanted in parishes where we used to have to endure hearing that dreadful agony called Gregorian Chant! Oh yes, these servants of ours have the whole Church in a wonderful state of confusion and turmoil, and all the while, we reap souls as if there is no tomorrow because they are so busy with their New Age agendas instead of preaching that horrid old message of sin, repentance, and the sacramental life which we hate so much. What a time to be a demon, when we can actually have baptized humans in our Enemy's Church living in open rebellion against everything that the Church stands for and teaches. And that we have bishops and priests who join in on this delightful little pastime of theirs is a joy to every darkened heart in hell.

There was a time that such men would have been slapped across the face – like our servant Arias at the Council of Nicea – and thrown out on their ears! And little do these insolent rebels know that with each passing day, their sin makes them harder and harder against the truth that could save them from wrath, until at their last day, they will die unable to even cry out for mercy because they will be so hardened. This is our work, my evil young nephew, not making men sin greatly, but making them sin those small sins of pride and rebellion over and over again, until finally they have hearts as hard as concrete against our Enemy. It may surprise you to know that the great sins are actually bad for our work. Great sins can so shock these insects that they fall on their faces crying out in real repentance. Then our Enemy, never missing a chance, rushes to their piteous cries to fill them with all sorts of graces in response and they are almost completely lost to us. No, great sins are wonderful fun to watch, but really cause us more problems than they are worth in the long run.

(As an aside, let me say that great sins are wonderful in pagans. They do a much deeper and quicker work of hardening, with much less chance of your having to deal with sorrow or repentance. If you have a little free time, study the Aztec civilization to see how this worked.)

What a marvelously confusing testimony this rebellion is to

those pagans and Protestants who actually trouble themselves to look at the Church and consider converting. I remember hearing one African pagan say to another that in his opinion, Christianity is a religion of fools and the mentally deficient. I would probably feel the same way if I observed what is passing today for Christianity. Even pagans know that you do not profess to be the friend of your god, and then oppose everything he teaches through your chieftains.

But a convert is a danger even to these, our people inside the Church. Therefore, this <u>must</u> be nipped in the bud and quickly. If you value your safety, and like being in a pain-free existence, you shall take immediate heed to this warning and get busy <u>now!</u>

I have formulated a plan since our last correspondence. Since he has become so enamored of those pestilent Early Fathers – give him what he wants! Yes, inundate him with their writings. Just be sure that you go to special care to see that he reads conflicting statements on doctrine from several different Early Fathers. Direct his attention away from unity of thought to see the differing interpretations on the same passage of our Enemy's Book. Do this especially with the Eucharist, in which he has become so disgustingly interested. Take quotes from them completely out of context so that he thinks that the Early Fathers did not have a united belief in the Real Presence. He is far too early in his investigation of the Enemy's writings to be able to resolve such problems, and if they are used correctly, we can get him back safely into his comfy Presbyterian pew with hardly any damage done at all.

Yes, sow doubt and sow it well. Always remember: doubt well used is a demon's best friend. You will be amazed at where just a bit of it, judiciously and properly used, will take you in your labors! Be sure you water your doubt with other confusing messages. You do well to use as fertilizer some of the latest writings by theological liberals such as Richard Rohr or Ronald Rolheiser. How nice that the Enemy's bishops don't appear to have the testicular fortitude to insist that such writings be burned like they did with that wonderfully horrid mess of a translation William Tyndale made of the Enemy's Book. Of course, what I even more enjoyed seeing was them burning Tyndale himself, although we lost a fine servant when he went up in smoke! Anyhow, if you do this well – and I have every confidence in your abilities – you will raise up a lovely plant of doubt that will absolutely blot out the sunlight of Truth to his mind. Then we can move on to further your training.

Once you have raised up this plant, the secret to success is this: do not neglect it! See that it is properly cared for. I can't tell you how many novice demons I have watched do a good job of completely confusing their subject, only to leave the job undone by turning their attention to other matters. You simply cannot do this. Your finish work is every bit as important as how you begin with one of these pestilent creatures. They are just too curious for our good, and despite having the intellect of a slug, those creatures do have the ability to reason – a most disgusting ability our Enemy has given them – and they will often spend hours as they drive or sit around, pondering the concepts that confuse them. Ofttimes they will actually, with the unfair addition of a bit of grace from our Enemy Himself, be able to think their way right out of our cleverly constructed traps, and find their way to the Enemy's camp. So I am warning you now, you must see this all the way to the end, and be very sure that your subject is left so completely dazed and confused that he runs back to the comfort of what is familiar – his Presbyterian assembly. Familiarity is comfort, and comfort feels like safety. We want him back where he feels comfortable.

I would also suggest that you that have our boy go to his Presbyterian pastor for a little talk. You see, he thinks that his pastor, being seminary trained, is familiar with the writings of the Early Fathers and can therefore be of help to him. He looks up to his pastor – almost idolizes him – because of the amount of knowledge his pastor seems to possess. (Remember, a few fancy high sounding words go a long way in keeping pew slugs mesmerized by their teachers!) Little does he know that not only did his pastor never even study the Early Fathers, (he was too busy actually memorizing that worthless Westminster Confession of ours – Priceless!) but he is as virulent and bigoted an anti-Catholic as ever walked the earth.

You can absolutely count on this pastor to go to do a heroic job of showing him how the Church was "paganized" by Emperor Constantine in the forth century. He may even drag out that glorious publication of ours, ROMAN CATHOLICISM, by Lorraine Boettner, and run through some quotes from it. I know it's on the third shelf of the bookcase in his study. You be sure he finds it during this talk! He will proceed to convince our boy that the Church was paganized to such a degree that the Enemy's Book alone is the only trustworthy guide. Typical Calvinist balderdash that we love so much to hear! Such pronouncements, coming from such a reverenced and lofty position as a pastor, are wonderful fertilizer for doubt, and should end any further consideration of the Catholic Faith. I know because I have used this tactic before and it is a sound remedy for this possible apostasy from our camp.

As an aside, I must say that I find it howling funny that the same Protestants who claim that the Church is filled with pagan errors absolutely bow down to and worship a book which was both written and canonized by these same "paganized" Catholics! They will strut around, thump their Bibles with ferocity and a gleam in their eyes as they tell their fellow ants that the Bible teaches against the Catholic Faith, while all the time they are completely ignorant that it is Catholic written and canonized by men who were supposedly filled with "pagan ideas."

Imagine that – holding a Catholic Book in your hands and claiming that it teaches against the Catholic Church! To listen to them, one would think that the Bible created the Church instead of the Church drafting the final canon of scripture at the Council of Carthage! Oh ignorance – what bliss you are for us!

You can also use his church friends in this campaign. Choose them with care. Use only those select ignoramuses who in their bigotry think nothing of what anyone else ever taught, who know little to nothing of our Enemy's true teachings through the Church, and whose pride will not allow them to shut up from showing off the erroneous little they actually do know. These kind talk and talk and talk and love to cover their ignorance by the use of the aforesaid high sounding words, which are meant to be very impressive to those who hear. That is how you can recognize them. Loudmouthed, windy blowhards who think, deep in their pride filled little hearts, that they are smarter than anyone who ever walked the face of the earth. Why, if only everyone would just listen to them and their fine theological ideas, the world would be a new place by next week! They are among our best friends. I find myself constantly in stitches listening to their vapid banter. They brag about being Bible only believers, but listening to their explanations of that Book is like listening to a three year old human explain nuclear fission. Whenever I need a little pick me up I just tune in to one of them and find myself rolling on the floor for the absurdity of their intellectual emptiness.

I have given you many tools to work with. A wise demon will use them all and overwhelm his subject so that no resistance can be put up. Do this, do it well and as I have instructed you, and I shall put you in for a small commendation with honors once he is safely returned to our fold. Believe me, it will be a most delightful fun for you to watch his budding interest in the Enemy's Church collapse in ruins around him.

Oh, and for hell's sake, lose that idiot Email address you have! I do hope that was not *your* idea. It is beginning to give me grave doubts about your abilities.

In service to hell, I remain,

Your Uncle, Infernus

CHAPTER THREE

From: darktormentum@ lake_of_fire.org

To: screamingtorture@ tormentmasters.com

Nephew of mine –

Well, at least now your Email *sounds* like you mean to hurt someone. If you were trying to flatter me with false student/master humility, it didn't work. What is the fascination you have with old Chinese martial artists, other than they knew how to shed copious quantities of blood and gore? I guess to each his own hobby, although yours seems most bizarre to me.

I commend you on your first effort. It was actually quite entertaining to watch, and I shall give you a passing grade on both your effort and on how well you crafted the whole scene! I do appreciate that you invited me to drop by and critique your efforts. In the busyness of my duties I had forgotten that his pastor is also an ex-Catholic! The entertainment of that night was well worth the inconvenience of your wretched hovel.

What a dressing down! Rarely do I see such amazing good form used in tearing apart, denying, and outright insult of our Enemy's Sacraments. To borrow a little from your fascination with Chinese martial artists, his pastor is a Kung Fu master in the art of completely misinterpreting the enemy's Word. He just absolutely stripped it of any meaning or importance at all in the life of the Enemy's people! I note our boy was a little surprised at the level of contempt shown for Ignatius and Augustine, especially since Presbyterians cherry pick what they like out of Augustine's writings. That's the fun of having humans be polite and hide their hatred for the Church – when it finally erupts it is absolutely spectacular! Fourth of July fireworks aren't as good as it was to watch the selective anger this pastor expressed so eloquently against the Church.

Of course, it helps us so much that the Church practically went to sleep in the last 200 years. Poorly catechized Catholics make the best converts to our cause! They read our publications, listen to our servants, and then convert and actually think that now they really are serving the Enemy! Gaaaaaaaaak.... excuse me, I am laughing so hard I am choking. And they are so easily made to hate the Enemy's Church! There is absolutely no hatred for the Enemy's Church like the hatred of a former Catholic who has abandoned the faith for what he considers to be "real Christianity."

Why?
You ask why?

Why, my infernal Glimslug! I am *more* than a little surprised that you don't know this! What in hell has that Academy of ours come to these days? I think I need to make a little inquiry after this session is over and find out who has been instructing you before you came under my glorious tutelage. Either we are allowing miscreants to teach, or you were napping when you should have been taking notes.

This foundational hatred by ex-Catholics against the Enemy's Church has one main source – fear of damnation. It is specifically because you are talking about the eternal destiny of souls, and believe me on this if nothing else, such is no small matter to ones such as our pastor friend. When they think of spending an eternity in the lake of fire, they become very emotional. Add to that the thought that they almost went there because they imagine the Enemy's Church taught them falsehood ...well, that makes them almost apoplectic. And then, when they think of their dearly departed grandparents, or a mother and father, being tormented in hell forever just because they are Catholic – they become absolutely haunted. The mental images of Grandma and Grandpa in hell (which a wise demon will be <u>sure</u> to constantly refresh in their minds), suffering, tormented, and screaming, (remember that sermon by our good friend, Jonathan Edwards?) why, they become absolutely livid with rage that the evil Catholic Church would send Grandma and Grandpa to hell with its false teachings. How could they not hate this Church, which in their minds was responsible for their loved ones suffering forever?

This fear and loathing are how they become _ours_ in their hatred for the Enemy's Church and the Truth She teaches. It is just too good!

We have no better soldiers in our ranks than ex-Catholics. Legendary are the deeds and exploits of these warriors in pulling Catholics out of the Church. They learn every trick, memorize every single piece of our misinformation, study and restudy every misinterpreted verse of the Enemy's Book, and are absolutely tireless in witnessing to Catholics to get them "saved." Not even physical violence will stop them. I only wish they would leave our pagan tribes alone. There is nothing I detest more than a nicely religious Hindu, Buddhist, or Muslim hearing about that accursed Cross for the first time. Some of them even believe and submit to baptism, and as we know, that is enough to save them, even if they don't know a nickel's worth of theology, or where to find the Gospel of John in the Enemy's Book.

What is even more dreadful is when some of these converts actually find our Enemy's Church, through study or some other means, and apply to become members of the True Church. Ugh! Utterly distasteful. But, I guess even hell is not perfect – we take what we can and do the best we can with it.

So, this is all well and good, but now we must follow success with success. It is not enough to simply destroy this budding interest in the Church, which you appear to have done quite nicely – he looks soooooo confused, poor little dear! – but let us now use the tools we have at hand to build him into another monster of hatred against our Enemy's Church! One more totally sold out to our side – how wonderful that will be, especially in light of the disgusting spectacle I was forced to observe last week.

Of all the days on the calendar those creatures use to mark time, I must admit that I far and away _hate_ Holy Saturday the most. Not only did the Enemy Himself enter into the very halls of hell on that wretched day and mock our Master as He led away the souls we had trapped in Paradise, but every Holy Saturday after that we have had to endure watching scores – scores, I tell you! – of turncoats betray us and leave our clutches! It is enough to make one violently sick.

This past Holy Saturday was no different. Yes, we have slowed down the number of converts to the Enemy to a virtual trickle, thanks in no small part to the fifth columnists we have strategically placed in the Church, but I want it to stop, and I mean now! I live for the day that not another soul even thinks of the Enemy and we reap them nonstop into our Master's clutches for His dreadful amusement. I was forced to watch two of my subjects – my own subjects! – not only leave my authority in an act of defiant rebellion, but curse our wonderfully dreadful Master, and spit at the mention of his name as they did so. I had settled them years ago comfortably in their little pews and filled their heads with all kinds of pap and nonsense against the Church. There wasn't the slightest hint from either one of them that they had any interest in the Enemy's Church. I saw nothing amiss from day to day and then all of a sudden, out of the clear blue, they pledge loyalty to the Enemy and vow to never obey any of us again, including the Master himself.

In all my days as a tempter of souls have never experienced such a remarkable display of hidden interest in the Enemy's teachings. How could I have known that both of them would find the Enemy's Church just by reading that accursed Book of His and nothing else besides? I thought they were just studying to reinforce themselves in the errors in which we had them so well schooled. And then – BANG! – out of the clear blue they go to Fr. Martin and tell him *"I want to convert to the Catholic Faith."*

Arrrrrrrrrrrrrrrrrrrghhhhhh! I'll convert you! Into a smoking piece of human meat sausage, you traitor!

They would be stunned to know how lucky they are. If it wasn't for each of them being protected by their own guardian angel (how *do* those angels get so big?) I would have personally rained hell fire on both of them for such rank insubordination and treachery against our unholy cause! And mark this well, the Master was no little bit unhappy about it. I still do not quite understand how I am not even now screaming in torments for such dereliction of duty regarding these two. I could have sworn I had them both well in hand, especially that male I had hooked on pornography.

Ugh! What a horror! He has begun to receive that accursed Eucharist and now finds himself so united to and filled with the Enemy that every chain of pornography has broken off him and he is as free as a bird. That is why we hate the Eucharist so much. Received in faith, it conveys the Enemy's grace and power right into the souls of these dullards. They throw off our chains and revel in freedom from sin. If we can't keep these ants in error, then the next best thing is to have Catholics who believe they are just receiving bread and wine and not the Enemy Himself. That way they have no power against sin and we can even reap them into hell right out of the very pews of Enemy's Church! Why do you think there are so many sinful Catholics out there whose lives are completely unlike the Enemy? It is because they have come to a point where they don't believe a word of it. Church is just a nice social function for them on a Sunday morning – something that Mom and Pop taught them to do. They may show up, but they don't believe word of it, and that puts them right in our clutches. Sacraments without faith are *worthless!*

Regarding your subject, nephew, I believe that one more meeting with our pastor will set the seeds of doubt firmly in the good soil of confusion. Seeing our pastor's love of absolutely scalding in boiling wrath anything Catholic, it should also provide a modicum of amusement in the midst of this depressing season when we have to tolerate the defections from our noble household. Be *very* sure that your boy doesn't stumble into one those new converts as he goes about his daily rounds, especially that Miss Simpson who was of late in his very assembly. I warned Trughnarf that she was becoming unstable in our teachings and that she needed remedial work, but he ignored my warnings, much to his painful displeasure. The only bright spot in that seamy affair is that she made absolutely no noise upon her departure. It is perhaps that wonderful emotion called shyness which made her keep her discoveries to herself, and thus minimized the damaged we suffered. She simply one day stopped attending the assembly. One such defection from the work of a novice demon I can somewhat tolerate, although I hate it. Ten would fill me with a rage that you have as of yet not seen, nephew.

We do not wish your subject to think of her at all, therefore be very sure to adequately fill his spare time with suitable distractions such as the chances of his baseball team making the World Series. (Will you please start using some of the tools we have given you?) He hasn't got a clue that she would provide not only a sympathetic ear to his inner turmoil, but some half decent apologetics, even for such a shy and mousey little nothing. I hate a well armed opponent, and she is giving every sign of becoming a real nuisance to us. Even the most insignificant of them can cause great harm with one well placed verbal salvo in defense of our Enemy's cause. I much prefer that those in the Enemy's camp be a massa damnata of blissful ignorance– stupid, uncaring, and quite lazy about eternal issues. In other words, typical Catholics. What a fear I have that some day they will start putting in as much time learning the Enemy's scriptures and Catechism as they do watching that vapid AMERICAN IDOL program on TV (how ironically and wonderfully named).

If they ever do that, we will be out of business in America in short order! They will take their religion seriously and absolutely destroy all the work we have done, from the White House right down to the lowest dogcatcher in Podunk. Our pro-abortion politicians will be out looking for work, our liberal priests and bishops will be howled out of office, and these slugs will commence to live as the Enemy wants them to instead of as we have them living.

Can you imagine them actually living in such a way that they refuse to start wars for profit, refuse to kill babies for profit, refuse, in fact to do any of the things we have them doing for profit right now? Imagine money becoming so unimportant to them that they stop printing pornography, stop putting our filth on TV, stop doing all the things we have them doing as they bow down to the almighty dollar in groveling fear. It gives me cold trembles to even consider such an event. By all that is evil in hell, may such a thing never, ever come to pass!

Of course, one bright spot is that even if we were to suffer such setback in America, we would still have the French, who now pride themselves on being too intellectual to actually believe in and obey the teachings of the Church. They are such typical Catholics of this age. The few who actually attend go mostly for the sake of appearance, then go home and fornicate with their neighbor's wife. Hot hell, I love that! No wonder observant Protestants aren't interested in the Church when they see a consistency of behavior like that! You can give those Protestants one thing – which we use against them when they look at the Enemy's Church – the majority of them are pietistic and moralistic, and our lovely sins, practiced by wicked and uncaring Catholics, offend them right down to their shoelaces. That's one major reason we do not have to suffer far more defections than we have seen lately – Catholics behaving like anything but Catholics! We have so many good and unwitting supporters in this. There is simply nothing finer than to have a cussin' and drunken Catholic right next to a devout Protestant in the work place, especially if that Protestant is your personal subject!

Another equally bright spot for us is that now, after decades of effort on our part, the Spaniards are finally opening the doors to our abortion franchise, ensuring that thousands, perhaps millions of them, will murder their way right into our arms in the name of so called "women's rights." We can make space for them right beside their cultured French neighbors, and they can spend their time spitting on each other between howls of rage and torment. How wonderful it has been over the centuries to watch these Christians hate and kill each other just because they are of two different ethnic groups. You must have heard the story of how Globscumus was promoted to Darkness Major by his creation of the eternal dislike between the French and the Spanish. So many wars between them – so much fun! He has filled hell with the souls of the self-righteous on both sides who went to war in the Enemy's name – the One Who calls Himself "The Prince of Peace" (isn't that just wonderful irony beyond words!)

Well, the Prince of Peace He may be, but His supposed subjects have had precious little to do with His teachings in that area! They were such fine Catholics that they killed each other by the thousands at the slightest behest of kings and emperors who were Catholic in name only.

All the better for us! War is the best tool we have for taking the enemy's citizens right out from under His nose. How easily these simple vermin are offended by each other. How quickly they lose all sense of their baptismal vows by which they promised to follow their Master in the ways of peace. Oh no! A little insult, a simple slight, and they are ready and more than willing to kill each other for their honor or some other equally vain pretext. In a war, even the best of them can be prodded to the point of breaking and committing the most vile atrocities. Then, we have him!

How, you ask?

Very simple. Guilt!

The wise demon will remind the retired warrior daily of what he did. They call it Post Traumatic Stress syndrome. It appears that for any of these insects with even a tad of morality, it is highly stressful to have to endure daily memories of setting fire to a whole village full of innocent citizens. Somehow, the Enemy has made it very hard for these creatures to kill each other, so that when they do run over His moral restraints, all kinds of wonderful things happen which can only benefit our cause.

Yes, the wise demon gets right into his subject's mind and reminds him daily of how he destroyed another life, of the ungodly hatred and rage he felt, how he attacked the image of the Enemy in another creature. Mental pictures of innocent civilians, especially children burned and maimed, are especially good for turning up the guilt and inner turmoil. Before long a demon can destroy a subject's mind, drive him mad, and make him lose all hope, especially in obtaining any of the Enemy's mercy. Best of all is when one of these fools commits his soul to us by an act of suicide. We just win, win, win in a war.

Even if we cannot get one of these pests to kill himself, more often than not, we get to watch him destroy his family, for while the businessmen who are profiting hand over fist from the war (How I love the military/industrial complex!) are patting him on the back and telling him what a great patriot he is, he is becoming moody, morose, and an absolutely miserable father and husband. Guilt is so wonderful, and even the hollow accolades of patriotism cannot wash that away. Do I have to trot out the wonderful statistics on divorce among military families, especially those who have seen war? Luscious! A fine slap in the face to that wretched Sacrament called marriage, which I particularly hate!

It grows late now and I must go. I have a fresh new shipment of subjects – 5 horrified atheists, 2 pagans, and 2 wonderfully corrupt old Catholic bishops – who all need to be tucked into eternal fire forever. Be quick now about your business and we shall soon enough lock up your boy to join them!

With gleeful malevolence, I remain,

Your Uncle Infernus

CHAPTER FOUR

From: darktormentum@ lake_of_fire.org

To: screamingtorture@ tormentmasters.com

Nephew Glimslug –

Well! I must say that caught me quite off guard! I can't remember the last time I have seen such a thing among those creatures, especially the stridently anti-Catholic ones. Imagine that pastor actually apologizing to and then sitting down with your boy to read and discuss those horrible Early Fathers. And then, to top off a completely wretched and miserable evening, to actually have a reasonably quiet discussion, even in disagreement, about what they read! Even though that pastor of ours despises it as papist nonsense, he insisted upon acting in the love of ......ahem......you-know-Who to your boy and treating him with respect. And now – this is beyond bizarre to me – this pastor of ours has actually become a tad curious and has in secret begun a study of the Early Fathers.

Nephew, I get the uneasy feeling that somewhere along the line our Enemy has once again played unfair with us and given this one a small dose of grace to see what he will do with it! Shrieks and Torments! I am rarely wrong in reading a situation like this, but this appears to have been a major foul up on my part! What I would give to have that omniscience the Enemy has. I certainly would have seen that coming and would have given you other and much better advice. There are always a number of ways to defeat these creatures and bring them home to our Master. How could that have been such a wrong course of action when it looked like the perfect response to your subject's illegitimate investigations?

Well! Now we have two problems on our hands. Since I created this mess with my advice, which you obeyed to the letter, then I must now become personally involved in its remedy. When I come to you, please observe all Ido with close attentiveness. I did not attain the rank I have in the underworld by being an impotent and craven coward in the face of difficulties. Hell is filled with my victims, many of whom required long and tedious work.

It has been a good while since I have been out on the front lines in our Master's business. Rank has its privileges, but personally attending to and enjoying the destruction of a human soul is not one of them. I have been too long training novice demons and it will do me good to once again feel the thrill of battle and once again reap souls for our Master. And I *shall* get these two back to where they belong! You may count upon that! I can practically hear you asking of me how I shall reverse this damage, since both are now involved with books of quotes from the Early Church. Nephew, this one will be all too easy. Some night, when our pastor friend has put in a long day and is tired, I shall distract him so that he leaves these books out and in plain sight of his wife, from whom, up to this point, he has secreted them.

Wives, wives, wives! How wonderful they can be to our cause! They area rich resource, and you must use them wisely, and in a timely manner. There is nothing like a screeching, hysterical wife to dissuade the prospective convert from further investigation. Some of their hysterics are absolutely brilliant! I couldn't do better if I had made them up myself. I think my all time favorite is

"I WILL NOT BE A PAPIST'S WIFE!!

screamed at the higher levels of vocality. (How sad when I think of the first one who ever used that lovely phrase. Her husband had nerves of steel and patience to match. Lost to us forever, and eventually with the wife, no less! Ah, well!)

Of course, if the children are old enough, we can get them involved as well. Imagine the horror of a teenager to find out that dear old Dad has some sort of interest in things papist. The wise demon simply takes this information and paints vivid and lurid pictures in their minds. What will the kids in the youth group say if they find out? Oh, that is so precious – peer pressure! We use it all the time to advance our drug and pornography franchises, and we use it to scare the heaven out of kids whose parents are looking into the Enemy's literature. Nothing is so valuable to a demon's cause as a good round of peer pressure well applied.

Use family members as well. Don't ever forget about them. Except, of course, in this case. We want to keep our pastor away from his family members since they are all extremely loyal to the Enemy's cause. Stupid, theologically bright as a bucket of dirt – but loyal. As I told you before, our greatest ally has been the complete lack of quality Catholic catechism in the last 150 years in America. We in the infernal under regions need to be sure that this outstanding status quo is maintained for generations to come.

His whole family is Catholic because....well.....because they are Catholic. It's not for any reason of having a deep understanding or appreciation of the Catholic faith. They are hardly struck with anything even resembling awe for what the Enemy did on their behalf. Ungrateful louts! Why, the Eucharist is hardly halfway down their gullet before they are bolting for the doors and rushing home to gorge on ham or roast beef, and then plop down in front of the TV. Either that or they are off to the local mall looking for one more silly and worthless trinket to add to their already bloated lives. The real treasure for them – the gems in our Enemy's Book, praying the Rosary – they avoid like the plague. You can know how easy it is to deal with a family like this just by measuring the depth of the dust on their copy of the Enemy's Book.

And devotional literature? Pffffffffffft!

Forget it! They can recite to you every episode of – oh, what is that lovely little smut-filled TV program we started last year – DESPERATE HOUSEWIVES – but they wouldn't know a quote from St. Thomas Aquinas regarding the holy life if it walked up and slapped them in the face! Oh yes, I like them like that – fat, dumb, and happy. Totally self-centered. Letting your pastor raise too many questions around them might not only bring him back to the Enemy, but turn them into distinctly unpleasant creatures, the kind with which we do not like to deal. So you shall see that I keep him far, far away from them.

How, you ask?

Oh, that will be fairly simple. You see, as noisy and persistent as he has been in telling them that they need to *"get right with _ _ _ _ _"* (Well, you-know-Who) and how enduringly – over and over and over again – he has absolutely <u>trashed</u> with insults the Catholic faith to their faces, let's face it, he would be embarrassed to death to admit to any of them even a passing re-interest in the Catholic Faith.

Never forget to use emotions on your behalf and against these dull witted creatures. Hate pride, lust, (my favorite) embarrassment, sloth, and a host of others are the great weapons we have to keep them from doing what is in their own best interest. Take, for instance, the last subject I worked with, the one that got me this cushy desk job. A mere slight, an overblown sense of pride, and a spark of unforgivenness against his brother, delicately kindled over the next forty years into a roaring fire of bitterness, was all it took to get that one down here, along with a significant number of his followers.

Of course, our infernal Master noted with no small amount of glee that this man was a pastor to one of our assemblies. Noted also that he was looked up to by a great number of people, so that his fall not only destroyed him, but took with him a number of others. That is the kind of destruction that our infernal Master likes to see. Why just get one soul when you can play your cards right and get whole handful of them? The wise demon does not waste his time on single souls. No, he finds himself some human in a position of leadership and brings not only that one soul to perdition, but scores of deluded followers as well. Do you remember the Jim Jones triumph but a few years ago? How I wish I had orchestrated that one! Your great uncle Vomicus pulled that one off and he is now enjoying a high position of honor as a result of how that maniac deluded his followers and led them into hell in scores.

Politicians are also such great fun to deceive, especially the Catholic ones. It is beyond belief the way they will turn upon our

Enemy, whom they are supposed to love and obey according to their baptismal vows, and support our franchises the way they do. To watch the way they support abortion, unjust war, and corporate greed is luscious beyond my comprehension. These are creatures who are supposed to be faithful to their vows to the Enemy's principles, yet they sell their souls for a few dollars more than what we gave to Judas, and then spend a lifetime opposing the Enemy's Church at every turn.

In the end, thanks to these outstanding efforts by these unwitting dupes, we will reap millions of souls. Now, my nephew, that is working smart rather than working hard, and when you get your first Catholic politician in your hip pocket, you will assure yourself of a nice promotion. Our Infernal Master does take note of good work, and the deceiving of a politician is very good work indeed, but more so when that politician belongs to the Enemy's Church. It gives no small amount of delight to our dark Master to see the members of the Enemy's army turning on their Master like so many good Benedict Arnolds.

But I digress. Back to my most delicious story. This worm of a pastor was looked up to by millions on his TV ministry. He was revered as a great Christian and a deeply spiritual man, but not a whit of good that did him on the day of his death. All his fame, his supposedly being able to speak in tongues, his magazines, and all the other things he was involved in didn't help him one little bit on his deathbed. I can still see the look of disbelief in his eyes when I grabbed his soul and yanked it from that putrid mass of flesh.

"What's the matter?" I taunted him, *"Don't you remember that your Master said that unless you forgive others their sins, neither shall you be forgiven yours?"* I even quoted him chapter and verse of that accursed Book, just to hear the sweetness of his screams. And here he thought that just because he had accepted you-know-Who by making a verbal profession of belief in Him, he was bound for Heaven with no delay!

Faith alone! How I love that skewed and worthless idea we gave those Protestants! It is one of our best weapons we have against the Enemy's Church and to take people to hell. And to top it off, he even taught that nonsense to millions through TV, so that they are all going around talking about how surely he must be in Heaven.

Priceless!

Do you remember from your history lessons in Imp School what we did with Luther's writings on justification by faith alone? Wasn't that wonderful? We managed to reap huge numbers of Germans alive at that time. After all, my dear Glimslug, *they* were justified and assured of Heaven by nothing more than an intellectual assent to a bunch of facts. Why, without us even much prodding them, they actually came to the predictably false conclusion that because of this, they could do whatever they wanted to do without endangering their souls one bit!

And Luther – ah, he was such a grand help in the big scheme of all things. His statement about sinners being covered by the Enemy's righteousness like dung being covered by a blanket of pure, white snow was just classic! Of course, under that blanket, the German people were rutting like wild dogs in heat. All restraint was cast to the wind because they figured that if they were hidden from God's sight by this white blanket, well, they could do anything their base little hearts desired, and not answer to the Enemy! Germany became a moral sewer, an absolute pig stye of moral depravity. Lovely! Luther lived to see it all and rue the day he thought he was smarter than the Church. We filled the hell like never before. My hell, did we make our quotas for those decades! Of course, the Church was such a big help then, too. Corrupt bishops, prelates on the take, and that con artist, Tetzel, running around making promises he had no business making to shake the very last farthing out of the poor. Don't you just *love* greed?

The whole business was ghastly wonderful, almost as good as when we managed to get the Borgia family seated in the Chair of St. Peter. No wonder the peasants revolted when Luther blew his trumpet of 95 Theses! The Enemy taught people the virtues of poverty when He walked among them. The leaders of His Church at that time were teaching them the virtue of greed by their behavior. Sometimes our Enemy's Church has been its own worst enemy and all we had to do was sit back, watch the fun, and reap the souls! Do you know how many bishops/clorgy we have down here? There is a real truth to the saying that the streets of hell are paved with the skulls of rotten bishops.

I tell you, if I were that pope in Rome and was running the Enemy's campaign, I would never let any of those creatures advance to bishop unless I was absolutely sure they would never, <u>ever</u> question any of the Church's teachings!

And speaking of such fun things, my infernal nephew, I invite you to grab a chair and watch the fun as the maestro works! Pay close attention and learn from what you see. Perhaps you will have my job some day.

Some day when hell freezes over!

In anticipation of a hellish night, I remain

Infernus - Master Trainer

P.S. If you know what is good for you, you will not breathe a word – not a word, I WARN YOU! – to anyone about my little mistake with this subject of yours!

CHAPTER FIVE

From: darktormentum@ lake_of_fire.com

To: screamingtorture@ tormentmasters.com

Glimslug –

See?

Wasn't that easy? I like that not only did he rid himself of those obnoxious writings – he burned them! Burned them! Oh, a true Reformer this little fire lover! Just like his forefathers who burned Catholic priests in the name of God, and then had the nerve to expect a reward at the end of their miserable lives, thinking that they were serving the Enemy. Well, fire they loved and fire they have – forever! The Enemy may not step in to prevent His servants from being martyred for His cause, but He certainly does not forget those who did such things on our behalf. We have men down here now who *still* can't believe they were condemned for burning Catholics at the stake.

So now he plies his wife with flowers, profuse apologies, and an expensive dinner. Ha ha ha! How precious! If he's real lucky, he might get sex in another month. Honestly, this amazing female has gone above and beyond the call of duty. In my many centuries of service to our infernal Master I have seldom seen such verbal fireworks! But as much as I would like it if she cut him off forever, I will actually encourage them into bed tonight, as much as such behavior disgusts me. You see, if she is too harsh with him, we will have a bad blow back to deal with. He will go out and buy another set of those accursed Jurgens' Early Fathers books, but this time he will do a much better job of hiding them and reading them on the sly in his sacristy. We want just enough anger to scare him away but not so much that he figures that he has nothing to lose by reopening his investigation. So, with the help of a little too much Chablis, I will place in her mind remembrances of all that she found attractive in him, and shall spirit them off to bed for the night. When he wakes up he will be happy, he will be cured of his dementia, and we can move on.

Which brings us to our next issue – your potential convert, who is all too eagerly reading banned material again. Worse than that, he has now added a book of apologetics, Robert Sungenis' book NOT BY FAITH ALONE, and a good Catholic Bible, to the fray! We had him so well hooked on that sorry mess of a translation – the KJV 1611 AV –

that we could have kept him confused for a decade. There's just nothing like a bad translation of the Enemy's words to help us in our cause. I particularly love how the Reformers pulled the Apocrypha out of it. And now, five centuries later, its knucklehead proponents go about loudly claiming *"papists added those books to the Bible."* Haw! Isn't that just too ironic? They don't even know, the fools, that the first KJV ever published came with the Apocrypha. I swear, I just love private interpretation. How is it that we are so lucky as to get such a fine crop of lunatics like that?

What is that nickname by which they call themselves – Ruckman Knights? Is that it? Haw, haw! Ruckmaniacs is more like it. What a great help to our cause they have been. Do you know there are some of them who actually teach that the Enemy, when here on earth, preached from the KJV?

No, that was not a glitch in my computer! It's true! Can you believe these people would in the same breath say such nonsense and then trust that they have the intellect to read, understand, and properly interpret the Enemy's Book? In the face of the massive universe and timeless eternity, they actually think that they have the intelligence to properly understand the writings of the Enemy on their own! What incredible egos they have! Each one of them thinks he, and he alone, has a charism of infallible interpretation, which the Enemy promised to the Apostles alone. When I have a spare moment from attending to the souls of sinners dropping like snowflakes into hell, I like to watch them argue among themselves. Baptist against Presbyterian. Both against a Methodist. Then throw a 7th Day Adventist into the mix for even more fun and amusement.

I've observed two Fundamentalists – you know, those Bible thumpin' "KJV Only" types – hurling invectives at each other with a ferocity not seen in the trenches of their first World War. How charming to watch them both condemn each other to hell while I sit back here knowing that they both belong to me. Isn't that just wonderfully ironic? Of course, it isn't that both of them are theologically wrong that will send them down to us. Oh, no. The Enemy actually forgives, with that disgusting mercy of His which I will never understand, a tremendous amount of theological error on the part of the stupidest of these His creatures.

No, it is their sour, bitter, self-righteous and pride filled attitudes which is going to make them fall into hell like over ripe fruit. Just like our servants the Pharisees. Couple that with a wonderful fragrance of unforgivenness – that ancient vintage that Cain first tasted against his brother Abel – and they are doubly trapped and doubly ours. In all their supposed great Bible knowledge, which is about a thimble full in light of the eternal knowledge of the Enemy, they forget, or possibly don't care to remember, that our Enemy said that love covers a multitude of sins.

St. Paul (that apostate **bilge rat,** how did he ever escape our clutches?) made it even more clear in his letter to the church in Corinth that love is even more important than right doctrine. How many demons make the mistake of getting their assignments to focus in on doctrine and while filling them just chock full of errors, forget to disable their capacity for charity. Our Enemy has snatched away millions from us who were just steeped in our errors because they practiced a high level of charity. I don't think that to be particularly cricket of the Enemy, but until we take over and make the rules, we have to simply watch in absolute disgust.

Ah, but these Bible thumpin' Fundamentalists, like all types of fundamentalists in the world, can't begin to imagine that the Enemy would respect the ability to love. They hate the word "love" almost as much as I do. They make fun of it from their pulpits. To them, love means liberal mushiness and tolerance for anything, including evil.

Of course, theological and political Liberals have served us so nicely in this area by absolutely hijacking the word love, and making it a carte blanche excuse to accept and promote any and every evil. Church liberals condemn with harsh words those who point out evil, saying that they are "unloving" and "lack charity." Judgmental is another fine word they use. We have our liberal Protestant assemblies, along with some finely corrupted Catholic bishops, to thank for all that. To listen to their sermons (which, quite frankly, would gag a maggot) one would think they would welcome our infernal Master himself into their congregation – all in the name of love and tolerance, of course!

No wonder then that these Fundamentalists find the word love

52

so repulsive. If love means tolerating evil, then they want no parts of anything that even resembles real love, such as a charitable attitude towards those who disagree with you. To them, love is not as important as being a warrior for truth, especially if they see that love is a codeword for tolerating and even encouraging our immoralities. How easy it is to take such zeal and with the slightest encouragement, create yet another whole division of good servants who think they are serving the Enemy, when in reality their attitudes drive people far from Him and right into our Master's waiting arms!

For instance, that mean-spirited clan of ours from Kansas who run around with their signs protesting homosexual behavior at funerals. Aren't they just too wonderful? They honestly think they do service to our Enemy. The reality is that they are driving people away in droves from any consideration of the Enemy's message. And the absolutely hilarious thing about it is that they are telling the truth. Homosexuality is a slap in the face of the Enemy. He made those disgusting creatures, vermin that they are, to be just like Him – that is, to image Him in self-giving love and in that love to bring forth life abundantly. He is not sterile in anything that He does. Look at how His Creation just teems with life that is ever reproducing. Disgusting!

Bah! I hate life and I hate these creatures. The fewer of them the better, therefore, the best thing we can do is to convince them that such selfish, promiscuous, and sterile behavior as homosexuality is a perfectly normal and wonderful expression of love. I have to say, with considerable admiration for such stubbornness, that they are profoundly determined in their rebellion against the Enemy's plan – not even an epidemic of deadly disease has slowed them down one bit in their disordered passions. How wonderful for us. Our quotas get easier and easier to make every year, and yet the fools persist in behavior that will kill them and send them to us. Lovely! And with such good servants as Bishop Spong, and a host of other sycophants in high places, we should be able to keep this rebellion going for a considerable period of time.

It helps immensely, of course, that human beings no longer appear to feel shame. The Westboro Baptist crowd is nothing more than an expected response to homosexuals flaunting their disordered passions in the faces of those who find it repulsive behavior at best. This is understandable, but like good bigots, the Westboro crowd, who hate everyone, including and especially Catholics, don't know that charity would do so much more than hatred in delivering men and women out of our error and into the Enemy's Church. We need to keep that animus going, while at the same time making it look like the Church agrees with Westboro simply because She cannot accept homosexual behavior. Homosexual people, yes. The behavior, no.

But I digress. How did I get so far afield from my subject? Seems that my mind wanders more than usual lately. I must be getting old. What was the point I was about to encourage you to pursue?

Oh yes, your subject and his new studies.

Private interpretation. That will be the key here. Your subject has been very studious of the Enemy's accursed Word. Let us use pride and that scripture knowledge against him as we have done with so many others. There are several teachings of the Church which contradict everything he has studied so hard to believe in. He has spent countless hours learning these positions, going to seminars, and reinforcing himself in error. He is, in fact, a rather impressive specimen of expertise in our error, and his ability to remember all the scriptures we have given him.

Now use that against him. Carefully fill his mind several times a week with his favorite misinterpretations of the Bible. Guide his mind to open the pages of his new Catechism so that he opens to places which teach doctrines of the Catholic Church which he not only does not understand fully, but which contradict everything he has taught himself to believe. Then roll in the confusion and doubts – hard!

To aid in doubt, be very sure he meets old friends who love a rousing good discussion of theology. They will reinforce his error with gusto, ripping the Enemy's Church like so much paper. You will see that before long he will put down his studies in frustration. His ego simply will not allow him to admit that he and his wise friends could possibly be wrong about something so important.

That is what I just love about Protestants who fancy themselves exegetes of the Enemy's book – they imagine themselves to be brilliant scholars and everyone who has the nerve to disagree with them and the position they have chosen is considered a mindless boob. They even have the nerve to criticize the Ante-Nicene Fathers such as that slimy Polycarp who learned from St. John the Apostle. HA!

This is the advantage we have over these dull creatures. They study furiously, lock their teachings in place with what they think are irrefutable proofs, then seal the whole mess with the misbegotten idea that the Enemy Himself actually taught this to them by a direct revelation. This makes them almost invincible against Enemy agents who are well trained in apologetic warfare. No matter how well the Enemy's agent handles the Truth, no matter how good the level of apologetics, they will fall back on their ego every time, believing that they couldn't possibly have made a mistake.

Isn't pride a wonderful tool in the right hands? No wonder the Enemy puts it first on His list of deadly sins ahead of all other delicious evils. I must admit, that of all the sins we deal in, pride has a very uniquely special and wonderful fragrance. It is our greatest tool, and that is why I had you study it from the first lesson you took with me.

Do as I have instructed you, and we shall see an end to this matter once and for all!

With demonic deception, I remain,

Master Trainer Infernus

CHAPTER SIX

From: darktormentum@ lake_of_fire.org

To: screamingtorture@ tormentmasters.com

My evil trainee –

Well done, nephew of mine. I am pleased that you so well grovel at my feet and obey my authority and orders. You have succeeded quite well in once again clouding up the issues for our boy. I note strong indications of a remarkably dark career as I watched you and personally oversaw your work. Now I can report to our Dark Master that all is going well with our subject and not be in fear of a very painful reprimand. You do not know it, but this whole episode had me under a very intense and quite malevolent scrutiny. I am not the nervous type, but it has been a long, long time since I have experienced the Master's dark wrath and I care not to ever do so again. I now turn this subject back over to you, resting in a good sense of your growing evil competence.

Although this is cleaned up nicely and our boy is once again reading his Chick tracts – those wonderful, poisonous little packets of lies and absolute nonsense about the Catholic Church – we need to tidy up a few loose ends. This is <u>your</u> responsibility, so heed my advice carefully. The Master has freed me from further responsibility in regards to this whole incident, however, you still have a responsibility here. If you value your safety, be aware that danger still lurks about.

Our accursed Enemy still keeps placing thoughts in our subject's mind. We cannot have this. He has be brushing them away – the with help of the aforesaid Chick tracts and other lying publications – but we still need to be on high alert as long as this onslaught continues. One of them might take root and bloom into a weed most difficult to deal with. Better it be uprooted now, or even more to the point, not be allowed root at all. I suggest a strong diversion to keep these thoughts from finding root, and there is no better diversion than that of love. He will not be able to concentrate on stray quotes from St. John Chrysostom if his mind is filled with thoughts of some nubile young female. Believe me, he is at that age where his hormones are absolutely our best friends.

Intoxicate him. Gradually and delicately push every thought out of his mind except for the thoughts of the young beauty you shall choose and place in the path of his life. And if you can somehow manage to compromise his thinking and lead him into fornication – ahhhhh, all the much better! I will tell you up front that with one as pietistic as your subject, that would take the most delicate of touches, but guilt has such a wonderful destructive power over both the soul and the rational powers that it may be worth a shot. You could perhaps not only dissuade him from further investigation into forbidden territory, but could well destroy his entire misbegotten faith in the Enemy once and for all. And don't say it can't be done. I have seen monks and priests, men of singular strength of character, more holy and devout than our boy will ever dream of being, fall flat on their faces, ruined for life and eternity. All it took was a steady and persistent calling of sexual temptation. Like water that eventually erodes through rock, persistence is the key.

Yes, persistence! I have seen way too many demons give up after being chased by a single decade of the Rosary. Yes, it burns, and most unpleasantly, unlike the fire we enjoy down here, but you must grit your pointy teeth through it and come back with an even stronger temptation. This is war, man, and you don't tuck your tail between your legs and run at the first *"Hail Mary, full of grace"* that comes flying your way! You should see the scars that I have from some of my more well-known battles with Her over souls of Her children. Yes, She must ultimately respect their free will in all things, but what a fierce Protectress She is! She wields the power of that Son of Hers like a seasoned gladiator who has killed 10,000 lions. And heed this warning well – there is more than one demon whom She has seriously crippled with Her powerful intercessions to Her Son. Since you are still a novice, I would be very careful who you pick to thrust in our subject's way, and steer a very clear path away from any of Her female children. You are not at this time large enough, capable enough, or mean enough to take on even a small guardian angel, much less resist Her in all Her battle armament!

Of course, our boy presents no such threat at this time since he is not under Her care, being still of that mind set which says that prayers to Mary and the saints are nothing more than glorified idol worship. How lovely to see him ignore such a fierce Protectress, and such finely crafted weapons, in favor of his pathetic little prayers by which he tries to take us on by himself. Hilarious! What complete arrogance! Like bringing a knife to a gun fight. Of course, what is even more delicious than this – and you will grow to absolutely love this – is when we ourselves answer their vain and impotent prayers to the Enemy. We make them think that the Enemy is answering them. Of course, you can only do this with the prayers of the hypocrites, and our subject is not a hypocrite   at least not yet. But he certainly does not have access to those powerful Marian prayers yet, and we should strive mightily to see that he continues in such ignorance.

How I just love to answer the prayers of Charismatic preachers who have a mistress on the side. Or Baptist preachers who are generously helping themselves to the offering plate. And female pastors – oh, that is too easy and just too good. The more wicked these creatures are, the more they dive unrestrainedly into sin and rebellion against the Church, the less protection they can obtain from that soft-hearted Enemy of ours. More wickedness and rebellion on their parts equals more ease on our part in giving them everything their nasty little hearts desire, and then making them think they are getting it directly from the Enemy's hand. They then have the nerve to think that because they got their prayers answered, they are in good stead with the Enemy and His kingdom is their home. All the while they belong to us – lock, stock, and barrel. The greatest reward you can have as a demon is to be at their deathbed and see the look of absolute horror on their faces when they realize the truth of their lives and their eternal end!

Those Faith and Prosperity preachers, you know, the ones who call themselves the Name it and Claim it teachers, are an especially delightful group to deal with. They are spiritually so far from the Enemy's camp that you can give them just about anything their little hearts desire. Cadillacs, mansions, money, swimming pools – my hell, how insatiable their greed is! It is almost as if they never read that Book at all, especially where the turncoat Saul wrote *"having therefore food and raiment, let us therewith be content."*

Content?

Hahahahaha!! Not them!

They want everything, they want it all, and they want it now! What luscious greed! Why I have actually heard more than one of them file bitter and nasty worded complaints into the face of the Enemy because their greedy little prayers were not instantly answered.

Of course we don't answer them all right away. It is more than passing fun to watch their greed and their inner anger mount as they pray and we withhold from them all the things that they have set their hearts upon. If they had half a brain they would realize that the doctrines they believe in are right out of our pit, and contradict everything the Enemy taught when He walked on earth, but they are sooooooo dim. I like them that way, for it is much easier to keep them in line as they march towards their ultimate end with us.

What is even better is watching how upset and confused the true sons and daughters of the Enemy get when they see this happening. It shakes their faith right down to their core to see our subjects appear to have the Enemy answer their prayers. I could give you a long list of many of them who finally gave up in disgust, betrayed the Enemy, and came to live with us permanently over just this very thing. So get busy and answer his prayers. What I mean, of course, is send him some lithe little wench who will dazzle him and eventually seduce him because she is all religious talk and no morals. You can find this kind of woman anywhere.

If you can't do that, at least send him one who is distracting enough to keep his mind on her and off the Enemy's writings. That should be easy enough. A first day demon can pull that one off. He's young, his hormones are driving him crazy, and he, like all males of the species, likes nothing better than to have a female doting over his every word.

I shall check with you later to see how you handle this latest assignment. Have your books in order. The last time I checked them I was disturbed at how sloppy you have become in your record keeping.

With malevolent intent, I remain,

Your Uncle and Trainer, Infernus

CHAPTER SEVEN

From: darktormentum@ lake_of_fire.org

To: screamingtorture@ tormentmasters.com

Nephew Glimslug –

While we enjoy the spectacle of watching your subject brood over his general theological confusion and inability to understand even the most simple of Catholic theological terms, I think it would be a good time for us, before we return to further torment his already cloudy mind, to engage in some furtherance of your learning as a novice demon. So far you have done fairly well, yet I see some rough edges in your overall approach, and I think that further instruction, gleaned from centuries of bonding souls to our Infernal Master, would be most helpful to you on your journey into full demonship, and a place among the great tempters of the Underworld. After all, I do have a reputation to maintain as the _best_ and most worthy of all trainers in his Dark Majesty's service!

Your latest attempt to entice our boy with a pile of compliant and lustful female flesh was ....ahhhhhhhh.... shall we say, a bit over the top. I must say that on a certain level, I found it rather humorous to watch you run for the high weeds when he threw the Name of the Enemy straight into your face as you were standing there beside that nice young wench whom you enticed to make that rather salacious offer to him! Haw haw, that was rich indeed! You have the zeal for evil, nephew, but you lack the knowledge of how to apply your young infernal wisdom. You also are a bit ham handed with your temptations, and need to understand how to more delicately lead souls into ruin. So, let us go review some very basic knowledge designed not only to keep the inquisitive from ever developing a full-fledged interest in the Enemy's Church, but to ruin as well even those in our own assemblies.

1. Temptation is a delicate art with those who truly believe in the Enemy. Unlike pagans, you cannot just brazenly toss evil in their faces and expect them to lap it up like pigs in a stye. Even those who belong to the Enemy but are not in the Enemy's Church are very sensitive against doing wrong, therefore a fine touch is required with them. This is why we created the whole Protestant revolt in the first place. We simply had to create the idea in them that they could think for themselves, interpret that Book for themselves, and ultimately, decide for themselves what is evil and what is not. Once they began to think this way, then it was easy to bring to them very subtle thoughts which gradually took them away from obedience to the Enemy, and into various shades of rebellion.

2. Rebellion is the foundation of our existence, the basis of our lives, and our soul-damning goal for each and everyone of these silly sheep. But we cannot just induce them to revolt as our Master boldly did – face to face with the Enemy with a loud and defiant proclamation of rebellion. No, they would run from that. So we have used the Protestant Rebellion for centuries to get them to think they are serving the Enemy when in fact they are, in varying degrees, serving our Master and defying the Enemy by opposing His Bride, the Church.

Do you see how delicately that works? It is a masterpiece of deception by which we make these creatures actually think they are servants of the Enemy and yet give them over to serve us in our rebellion. The nice part about it is that there is a fine line of sin which they can cross without knowing that they have become ours forever. Your job is not only to keep your subjects in rebellion, but to delicately induce them over that line so that they no longer can escape us. As I told you before, small sins done repeatedly over a period of years have the effect of hardening their souls to Truth. This is why the Enemy's Church has, for centuries, warned Her subjects about venial sins. Of course, most of them are not listening nowadays, which is just fine for the success of our cause.

3. Lead with thoughts – follow with actions. *Very* important concept. This is where you got into trouble with that young wench you tossed at your boy. You might well have succeeded if you had spent a couple of weeks tenderizing him with a constant barrage of lustful thoughts and hormonal annoyances. You have to set up evil deeds with a foundation of evil thoughts first.

It's called temptation.....remember? You just tried to steamroller him. Very seldom does that work with those who believe in the Enemy. You have to use their darkened minds against them. The flesh follows the mind, not vice versa. If a man has safeguarded his mind, you can bother his flesh all you want to, and you might as well try to cure the ocean of salinity by spitting in it for all the good it would do.

Take, for example, Martin Luther. I tormented that boy's mind for years before suggesting that mistranslation of the passage in Romans to him. Once he saw my interpretation, I began to gently put suggestions into his mind. Subtle ideas that he was smarter than all the other clerics around, that he alone had found something that not only had they missed, but all the other generations of Christians before him as well. Little by little I took that small spark of pride and turned it into a roaring fire of egotism. There finally came a point in his life that if the Enemy Himself had appeared to Luther and spoken in defense of His

Church and Her doctrines, Luther would have corrected Him. He had become that hardened against the truth.

We did the same thing with Calvin, Hodges, Tyndale, Moody and a host of other lessers. None of them just woke up one morning and decided out of the clear blue to espouse our teachings. No! We worked with them day after day, putting thoughts into their minds, leading them to conclusions which opposed the Church and teaching of 1500 years of holy men whom we couldn't touch. We worked arduously to assure them by as many means possible that they were correct and the rest of the Christian world was wrong, especially the Catholic Church. Go back to the library on your day off and spend time reading Toadpipe's VICTORIES OF THE REFORMATION...Vol. 3, especially the chapter on building false doctrine. Not a big book – you can read it in a couple of hours – but it has tremendous information for you at this stage of your formation.

Remember this: the mind is your worst foe and your best friend. It all depends upon how you use it. If you allow one of these creatures to study Catholicism without opposing what he is doing, he will use his mind to cooperate with the Enemy's graces and get himself into the Church. On the other hand, if you are right there to sow the seeds of doubt, you can stir him up to oppose the grace of God, write off the Church as hopelessly in error, and even spend his life vocally opposing it to all who will listen.

Probably the best example of how well this works is what we

have managed to do in sixty years to defile that ugly Sacrament of theirs called Holy Matrimony. Once upon a time, the vast majority of men and women knew that sex was something special which was reserved for marriage. Those who served us by engaging in promiscuity were marginalized by the societies they lived in. It was understood that they had committed wickedness and that such behavior was not to be emulated nor lauded.

But in the early 1960's, a wise student of mine by the name of Pusglomus applied the principle I have just shared with you, and urged a reprobate by the name of Hugh Hefner to challenge societal standards by publishing a magazine with just the slightest hint of nudity – the female breast. Yes, there was scandal at first, but since the men of America were either spineless cowards, or secretly wanted to buy his magazine and hide it under their mattress, this initial salvo went unchallenged. Real men would have defended womanly virtue, and not only burned every first copy off the presses, but covered Hefner in enough tar and feathers to do a highway. But no, they let it pass. The more reprobate of them even used the 1st Amendment of their country's Constitution to justify the publication of this fine magazine. Good for us.

With great wisdom, Pusglomus worked slowly and patiently. Year after year the magazine hardly showed much more flesh than the initial issue had, yet something else was in there which was doing a far deeper work than just the showing of a little female nudity. Hefner sought out, and was also found, by every possible degenerate on this accursed little planet. They wrote article after article in defense of open sexual experimentation. Little by little these articles began to bend the will of the American public away from the sanctity of marriage. Playboy magazine has been the vanguard of a host of such wonderfully obscene publications which have over time eroded the American conscience and turned this country into a veritable sewer of fornication. Such insult to the Enemy! We have churches filled with people who go there once a week, say their wretched and hypocritical little prayers, and then head back home to their live-in lover. We are making our quotas almost weekly now, thanks to these beautifully subtle efforts so malevolently applied.

Now, **highlight this in your notes:** if Pusglomus had tried to introduce all at once the multitudinous varieties of filth we have swamped the world with at this time, he would have failed miserably. 1st Amendment or not, the leaders of America would have had riots in the streets to deal with. He was wise enough to just start a little ember of vice and fan it over years into the roaring inferno of filth we so enjoy today. Look at the wonderful results it has had, besides filling hell. Millions of marriages ruined, disease rampant and running wild, and human beings using each other in the most degrading ways imaginable. I wouldn't use toilet paper the way these beasts treat each other. What a joy to watch! I hate humanity and anything that can be done to make them utterly miserable is the most pleasant thing in hell to me.

And ultimately, I guarantee you, this is how we will eventually get the human race to exterminate itself – by using their darkened minds against them. Slowly, deliberately, and with great cunning, we shall deceive them deeper and deeper into the blackness of our dark intentions until one day, the whole planet will be a smoking ball of nuclear waste which will never support life again. It will be glorious – glorious, I tell you – and I can hardly wait for that day to come!

4. Use other Christians against him. Whenever you have someone begin to show even a modicum of interest in the Enemy's Church, you should begin a negative campaign in his mind. There are literally scores of books at your disposal – TRAIL OF BLOOD, ROMAN CATHOLICISM, MYSTERY BABYLON, Chick tracts, etc – which you can use to instill in a potential convert a high level of distaste for the Church. These books are all monstrous lies, filled with every conceivable piece of anti-Catholic drivel against the Church that we could put into the authors' minds to write, but your potential convert will not know that. All he will see is *"the Church killed 60 million people in the Inquisition"* or *"the Church is filled with pedophiles."* Wonderful tommyrot without an iota of truth about it, but sufficient in many cases to put a sudden and abortive end to illegitimate investigations of the Church.

5. Remember also that the Church would be ten times the size it is today if it hadn't been so filled with the bad examples of Christianity that we have been able to use against potential converts. Look at Chief Joseph of the Nez Pierce Indians. He converted to Christianity, but after he saw the fine way that Christian American politicians and soldiers were treating his people, he chucked the whole thing as a farce and returned to his pagan native beliefs. That's just one of many examples of how Christians have turned millions from the Enemy by their wicked behavior. Ghandi was interested in the Church until he saw how Christians he met were distinctly unlike the Enemy. It is said that he once went to a church of some sort and the usher called him a "kafir" and threatened to throw him down the stairs. Now isn't that just ducky! That ended Ghandi's interest in Christianity forever. And you can do the same with stories of Catholic atrocities. Use them discreetly and they can be an invaluable aid to you in keeping Protestants from abandoning our religion for that of the Enemy.

6. Every man has his particular weak spot. Learn to recognize each one for what it is and to use it wisely. With some, pride works nicely. Calvinists are particularly suspect to this. My hell, do they ever pride themselves upon their learning! Honestly, if they could take their brain out of their skulls, they would spend every night they have on their knees before it in worship. They are like those in that Book who are described as *"ever learning yet never coming to the knowledge of the Truth."* This is because their pride will not ever allow them to admit that they might actually be wrong. I'm telling you this right now – a Calvinist converting to the Catholic Faith is a greater miracle than raising the dead. You see, the dead can't resist the grace of God, but a Calvinist can. And do they ever!

For others, it is the fear of you-know-Who. I am not talking about the holy fear which that Book says is the beginning of all wisdom. I am talking about craven fear of an ever offended Deity Who is seen as being stern and implacable. People who think this way are like Luther. They cannot see the Enemy as love and as loving them personally, but are scared spitless that if they convert to the Catholic Faith they will lose their souls. To them, the Enemy is a demanding perfectionist whom they must please by having everything doctrinally correct. Zero them in on one doctrine they don't understand and you can easily keep them out of the Church forever in fear of losing their souls. They don't see the Enemy as love, and the wise demon does everything he can to reinforce that belief.

It is especially lovely to use their very own Queen against them. Every Christian until the 16th century knew exactly who this Woman is and how the Enemy so greatly honored and used Her to bring salvation to the world. But the Puritans, that wonderful bunch of braggadocios know-it-all's we raised up, took an absolute delight in pouring contempt and scorn upon Her, making it seem as if honoring Her would be to spit in the Enemy's face. My hell, did they somehow forget that this was His Mother? What dolts!

They ran around spouting off the Ten Commandments at every opportunity they could and yet seemed to forget the one that says *"Honor your father and your mother, that your days be long upon the earth which the Lord your God shall give to you."* Didn't they understand that if Jesus is the believer's Elder Brother, then that makes Her their Mother? How come they couldn't understand that She is the New Eve of the human race, created to stand beside Her Son, the Last Adam? These people were completely ignorant and yet they fancied themselves *great* theologians. And fortunately for us, they have muddied things up for centuries because people like your subject also think they are great theologians. They have modern Protestants so confused that all we have to do is to show them some flowery poetry from St. Alphonsus Liguori and they run for the deep weeds, all the while cursing what they think is the idol worshiping of the Catholic Church.

My nephew, always study your subjects well and when you find one who has these misgivings about that Woman, use the tools you have to drive him back to his little enclave of Fundamentalist misfits. The right tool used on the right subject will work every time. When you have a subject who is offended by the honor given to that Woman, do not waste your time giving him objections to the Eucharist from our Protestant heretics. Likewise, for an Episcopalian who loves that Woman, occupy him with atrocities the Church supposedly committed against English Protestants. Be wise, my nephew, and discreet.

7. Keep your subject isolated. You must not allow him to realize that he is making a journey that literally millions have made before him. He must think that his ideas of converting to the Church are strange, bizarre, and unheard of. Make him feel like an oddity among men with his desire to convert to that strange cult of idol worshipers. In this area, many pitfalls await the novice demon. The Internet can be a place of horror for us with all its convert forums, convert stories, and orthodox Catholic writings. Yet, at the same time, you can use it to even further isolate your target. If you steer your subject into a forum which is run by fellow Protestants, he may very well insulate himself forever against the Church, going day after day to meet with his fellow sycophants in heretical commiseration. If you are assigned a subject who has absolutely no interest in the Catholic Faith, such a forum can lock him forever into his obstinate denial of the Truth.

In closing, let me again remind you of what we are dealing with. These creatures have an ability to both think and reason, but they cannot come to Truth without the aid of the Enemy. Furthermore, they tend to regard all thoughts that come through their minds as having originated with themselves. This is our greatest ally in this war for their souls. Learn to place suggestions in their minds with the most delicate of touches, so that they think that they are really the author of the thought you shall give them. This gives you the advantage then of using their emotions against them. Let me give you an example:

I once had a youngster who was seriously interested in

becoming a priest in the Enemy's Church. From my study of him I knew that if he were to obtain ordination, he would be a major pain to the work I had so carefully cultivated in my district. Therefore, I knew I had to derail him, but because of his rather formidable mind, I would have to proceed with distinct caution and the most delicate of touches lest he realize what I was doing.

Once this lad reached adolescence, I began a very subtle and quiet attack upon his senses. I started it easily enough, with his accidental finding of a Playboy magazine carelessly tossed aside in the garbage. I managed to sear those pictures quite deeply into his psyche, and then, without too great a frequency, brought them back from time to time to entice him into solitary sin. At the same time, I placed thoughts in his mind that he was the most wretched of all fellows, unworthy of even thinking of the priesthood. I used guilt – sparingly at first, mind you – to make him believe that he and the Enemy were far apart and that the Enemy was displeased with him for his lingering on these thoughts. This was not true, of course, but these creatures are so emotional and wired so tightly that the merest suggestion can be the one which gives you a great victory. The deeper into guilt he fell, the further away from God I made him feel. Soon I began to bring these thoughts to him while he was praying or reading the Enemy's Book. What a delight to see the confusion on his face when I would drop a vivid picture of a naked female into his cortex as he was in the middle of a kyrie elesion.

Well, nephew, the final outcome of this all was that he never did enter the priesthood. Oh, he's married and has children today, whom I am even now working on for our Master, but he is nowhere near the threat to us he would have become if he had only realized that the random thoughts he kept having were not his own and did not represent his true self.

This is the greatest weapon we have against the Enemy. But as I said, and I cannot say it enough, be as delicate with this as one of these creatures as when they dismantle a live bomb. If I had blundered with my subject, not only would he now be a priest, but he may have come to understand our tactics and would be teaching others how to overcome them. This is the kind of problem you can create for yourself if you are not extremely careful.

I hope you heed well these lessons. Certainly if you expect to ever achieve any rank in the underworld you will have to put them to use and produce a fine crop of damned souls for our Master. I have given you tried and true methods. Now go out and use them and get that subject of yours settled once and for all!

In full service of deceit and hell, I remain

Your Uncle Infernus

CHAPTER EIGHT

From: darktormentum@ lake_of_fire.org

To: screamingtorture@ tormentmasters.com

GLIMSLUG!!!!!!

You screeching, no good, disobedient, ignorant, lazy, worthless, pus-filled, ridiculous, vermin ridden, excuse for a demon! I have never seen such a complete lack of dedication, such a miserable failure to obey orders in my life!! And to top it all off, you dare whimper in my presence *"I didn't know it was her because I was behind her."* Behind her and then you push her right into his path so that they practically bump noses. You really made sure he saw her, didn't you? What were you thinking? Were you out of your quota of seamy hookers for the month? Did your supply of slutty little teenage girls in miniskirts somehow dry up and vanish? The fact that she was wearing her skirt way below her knees should have been a dead give away, even from behind. But nooooooooooooo, you must have been in a hurry to get somewhere because you just shove her practically into his lap! I SWEAR TO YOU BY   ALL   THO ./0sdf...oo n n v a . . . . . s d f p 9 2 8 . . . . . . **E R R O R** . . . . . . **E R R O R** >>>>>>>>>>>>>>>>>. . . . . . .

     I realize it has been some time since my last writing. In the anger I felt writing the last paragraph you received, I managed to turn my computer into a smoking pile of junk. It should have been you instead. Fortunately for me, our Master had the Draft Save provision installed with Windows 7, so I am able to pick up from where I left off. So that I do not have to issue a request for a third computer, I am going to attempt to hold my temper, however, I warn you, do not underestimate the level of my anger at this point.

     Of all the women available in your city, you somehow manage to pick that mousey little Benedict Arnold, formerly of his Presbyterian assembly, who recently kissed up to the Enemy and took those horrid and unspeakable vows against us and our Master's kingdom! Do you have <u>any</u> idea what is going to happen to us when word of this gets back to the Master? If he is in a very good mood, for which you had better cast some particularly evil spells and call in some favors, he might only demote me to a street job and roast you over an open fire for twenty-five years!

Did you somehow forget to whom it is that we are enslaved? Have you forgotten his malevolent temper, his complete lack of sympathy for demonic failure, and his utter delight in hearing the screams of those whom he torments and punishes? The screams of other demons who have failed him are music to his ears, and I, for one, have no wish to join that particular choir.

A plan. We must have a plan and damned quickly! Our time is fast escaping us. You had better come up with a good plan, genius, or you can plan on being Miss Welcome Wagon for excruciating pain for longer than you care to imagine. I still can't get over it! You pushed her in his way– making her trip over that high curb – just because you knew that he had a thing for long brown hair, and you didn't even bother to look at her face to see who she was, you numbskull!

We had this boy in the palm of our hot little hands. He was ours, I tell you, _ours!_ Filled with doubts, confused, wondering about the Enemy's religion, up one day and down the next – a perfect candidate for a meltdown, and now he sits around with her down at the lake and they stare at each other with lovesick eyes while exchanging quotes from St. Irenaeus. Horrid, I tell you, just horrid!

And that doesn't even begin to describe how the Master is going to feel about this when this piece of bumbling lunacy on your part gets back to him! Worse than that, she is daily showing increasing signs of becoming a formidable warrior in the Enemy's army! Who would have thought that such a quiet little church mouse could mount such valiant and stout defenses against the best of our attacks? She wields that Bible like a broadsword, the very same one she used to misuse on our behalf!

And where did she learn that Greek? Did you see how she just absolutely dismantled the best of his arguments on Luther's forensic justification and made a joke out of it, all the while giving him that sickening little sweet smile that has him hooked worse than a bass on a Number 8 hook. Gads, what a horrible turn of events this is! Couldn't we at least be lucky enough for her to be ugly? This is just horrible. Not only is she devastatingly smart, profoundly well read, and has a memory for facts like a proverbial elephant, but she is what these creatures call cute, and he is smitten with her right down to his toes. Horrible!

I am only in this because you are my trainee, and that is only because your mother, my sister, went to the Master herself and convinced him, by means of a number of unspeakably wonderful vile acts, to put you under my tutelage. Had I known that I was going to be saddled with a bumbling idiot, a brainless babbler without a clue who would lead to my downfall, I would have run from you like Rosary beads and Hail Marys! Everything I have worked so hard for is about to crumble in my hands and the best you can do is to say you are sorry? Oh, sorry indeed I shall make you before they drag my carcass in front of his Infernal and Dread Lowness to try to explain this complete meltdown. Anyone with half a brain can see exactly where she is leading him, and I promise you that on the day he renounces the Master and joins the Enemy's camp, I shall introduce you to pain you haven't even begun to imagine. Our Master will make us rue the day we were whelped, you for what you have done and me for not keeping a close eye on you as trainers are supposed to do with novice demons.

I am going to go be alone to think of some way out of this, along with practicing any number of disgusting displays of craven fear, cowardice, and mortification, which may lessen my sentence enough to keep me from spending even a day in the deepest parts of hell where I shall have to join in with the screaming of so many I have personally deceived. You better hope to evil that when I get back I have formulated some sort of brilliantly devious plan to escape the Master's wrath, and that I myself am in a better mood, or you will find out just how painfully proficient I am in the use of fire as an instrument of torture. You are beyond lucky that you are my sister's whelp, and she was with you when I showed up at your doorstep, or I would have fire devoured you right on the spot! The only good thing about this whole disgusting spectacle was the thrill of watching her beat you senseless for your vile disgracing of our most worthy Master! I hope you remain in severe pain for weeks as a reminder to never again engage yourself in such a reprehensible act of treason.

In wrath and anger,

Infernus the Terrible

CHAPTER NINE

From: darktormentum@ lake_of_fire.org

To: screamingtorture@ tormentmasters.com

Nephew of mine!

What a fabulous welcoming home gift you gave to me upon entering your door, although I must say that it does have some hidden problems within it that I shall discuss with you later. Nonetheless, I never for a second imagined you to be the sort of demon that you have demonstrated to me in reaction to my last Email. Your response to my correspondence was priceless, although I am nursing a certain wary fear it may turn out to be ill-conceived, as I shall explain in detail as I write.

Where did you get the idea of throwing that mousey little witch under a truck and ridding us forever of her persistent and pestilent attacks on our wonderful falsehoods, lies, and errors? I'll grant you this, that was an extreme but truly effective response. I am still amazed that you got that drunken lout of a truck driver to be able to even maneuver that vehicle in his condition, much less navigate the streets which you suggested to his befuddled brain. It has been a long time since I felt the kind of sheer pleasure that I felt as I watched the replay of him losing control of his truck, running out of control over the sidewalk where she was standing, and smashing her into a bloody pulp. I just want to watch that again and again, it feels so good!

I thought I had come up with a pretty good solution to the mess we were in, but your response honestly makes me look like a bumbling minor demon on a first assignment. Not only did you rid us of a growing nemesis among the ranks of the Enemy's convert soldiers, but you have absolutely crushed our subject with doubts about the goodness of the Enemy. And as a bonus, that bigoted former pastor of hers, the ex-Catholic, spent an entire Sunday sermon telling his little flock of mind numbed robots that this happened precisely because.......well, let me use his own words, they are so, so eloquent:

He said, *"This is what happens when you turn your back on the covenant you make with God in baptism and kiss Satan's harlot church, the Whore of Revelation."*

Oh, now wasn't that just delicious?! Now there are forty five scared little souls – petrified out of their wits – who will never even begin to think about entering the Enemy's kingdom. He has them so terrified of the Enemy that they not only wouldn't consider anything

Catholic, but they are telling others the same thing. What a grand insult to the character of the Enemy that they would describe Him as if He has the same evil and putrid character as our malevolent Master. That is what I love about Calvinism.

Imagine – our Enemy, Who is pure Love, being described as one Who is always angry with mankind. How choice to hear Him described as One Who arbitrarily – and get this, for his own pleasure – damns souls to eternal torment with us. What kind of love is that which they describe? What a wonderful insult to His character to go about describing the Enemy as love – as love, mind you – and then in the very next breath, these mindless creatures insist that He sends unelect babies down here to us. (I could only wish that were the case – I HATE babies!). How I love hearing them so wonderfully desecrate His character among themselves. And to top it off, they feel so noble about it when they do it!

Marvelous!

Better than all that, sort of the creme de la creme of the day, one of that pastor's congregants was so horrified by his sermon that she drove four hours to the house of her good Catholic parents so that she could spend the day witnessing to them. She got to the point of absolute tears and wouldn't stop talking and badgering them until they accepted you-know-Who and promised to come to the Presbyterian church in their town next Sunday.

What a farce! Such Catholics! They don't even know that their baptism truly has made them part of the Enemy's Body and they don't know even the slightest counter argument for that Evangelical drivel we put out about accepting you-know-Who as your personal Lord and Savior. Wonderful. Now they are confused, which they should be, and we are on the verge of seeing a glorious defection from the Enemy's Church to our noble Master's service! Oh, that has such good potential, since they are yet another pair of uncatechized Catholic misfits who don't know the first thing about their religion. Social and family Catholics like the majority of them out there. I promise you this, they will get a rousing sermon on justification by faith alone from the pastor we have there. I will make absolutely sure of that! There is so much great potential here. We got rid of a trouble maker, have your boy on the run, and our pastor has been firmly solidified in his fear of the Enemy regarding anything to do with the Catholic Faith. This a good day.

And yet, my wonderfully evil nephew, I must now in all honesty toss cold water on this scene of distinctly evil darkness. As I told you earlier, there are hidden problems here that cause me more than a passing concern. Our Enemy sees and knows everything, and not even one of those dirty little rats with wings – a sparrow – loses a feather without Him knowing all about it. You know what this means, don't you?

It means that He permitted this all to happen. Didn't you at least find it passing odd that her guardian angel was somewhere off duty and it was so easy to set her up for the big hit? When you noticed that big, dumb oaf with wings was absent without explanation, it should have immediately occurred to you that things were not right and something was amiss. The Enemy saw it all, I tell you, and He could have stepped in from a thousand different angles – a dead battery in that truck, a bus hitting it before it came to her, the drunken lout of a driver passing out and crashing before he got to his target – yes, my nephew, this was actually much too easy, and that causes me a deep and grave concern. Surely things look as if they are going our way, and the future looks, at first glance, wonderfully dark and evil for us and our plans. But I am no young demon. I have seen this too many times before, and it causes a cold shiver to run down my spine. What is the Enemy up to now and, even worse, have we played right into His hands by your rash and quickly acted upon choice of responses?

Do I need to remind you of some of those horrible failures that at first looked like rousing successes for our cause? Turgidfroth had the brilliant idea of killing off all the first believers – those pesky Apostles and their followers – and he roused the Jews, and then the Romans, to mighty and noble deeds of murder. But instead of terminating forever the fledgling Church as planned, it scattered the remaining Apostles and disciples all over the earth and they took that pestilent Gospel with them! And we couldn't shut them up! The more they suffered, the louder they proclaimed. They made converts – we killed them – and their deaths made yet more converts! What is it about watching a martyr die that so attracts others to their cause? You would think it would scare them away in droves. Soon this pestilent religion of the Enemy was all over the earth, and the faster we killed them, the quicker they made converts. We killed one and a hundred took his place. What a glittering jewel of stupidity that was! We should have known, we should have figured out that something was up after the Enemy let us kill the first hundred of them without so much as a peep of opposition to our plans. But nooooooo.... we just kept killing them for three centuries and the Church got absolutely huge. I think we all so much enjoyed watching their blood run that no one stopped and said *"Wait a minute! Something's going wrong here! There's a thousand times as many of them now as there were a century ago!"*

Mugglump thought that he could destroy them by introducing pagan and foreign religious ideas into their worship. Not only did they smell that out and destroy those ideas in councils, it unified the Church more and more with each teaching because they defined the Enemy's Truth better and better. Instead of weakening the Church, each council strengthened it. Horrible! We sent Arias – the Enemy calls a council. We sent Sabellius. Another council. Marcion. Still another council. Every fine heresy we brought out was met with yet another council, which unified and codified the Church so well that by the time the Protestant Rebellion was sent their way, they were absolutely unfazed by it. They called Trent, blew right through our teachings, and moved right on. Another plan taken by our Enemy and used for His good.

Gads! Even the Protestant Rebellion, as glorious as it was in the beginning, eventually blew back in our faces. We were all too happy to get the first and second generation of converts from the Catholic Faith. That was easy. But we forgot about the Enemy's rule of justice and we soon begin to lose souls at an alarming rate.

You see, greater the amount of knowledge that these creatures have about the Church, the greater their sin if they rebel against Her. By the third generation, we had things so fouled up that most Protestants didn't have a clue, and the Enemy held them as guiltless for this. In order to commit a mortal sin, they have to have a clear knowledge of what they are doing, and none of those after the second generation had even a clue that the Enemy's Church really is the True Church. Thus, they were held to minimal guilt. Our Enemy even went as far as to accept as love their truncated and non sacramental worship of Him and looked not at the imperfection of their doctrine and worship, but at the love they had for Him. They spend a lifetime ridiculing and writing against the Church, and because they didn't know any better, a bit of time in Purgatory is all they get? Invincible Ignorance? Ridiculous! What kind of justice is that?

Men like Calvin and Knox knew this all too well. So tormented were they by the thought that they really might be rebelling against the Enemy's Church that they were easy prey for us to give them that unbiblical idea of an invisible Church to soothe their consciences. Oh, they never admitted it publically, but even after they came up with this theological novum, they were still extremely uneasy down deep in their souls where the outer conscience can't feel. That invention of an invisible Church may have given them a false sense of peace on the surface, but I watched their souls in their non public moments, and I tell you that they couldn't silence the dread sense deep inside that they had done something really bad, and it was going to blow back on them down the road.

The only good which came from that rebellion was that by opposing the sole source of authority and teaching on the earth, we managed to open a virtual Pandora's box of confusion. Just look at the wonderful results we have today. Thousands and thousands of little mini popes, each holding absolute sway over some tiny congregation of deluded sycophants who accept his personal interpretation of the scriptures. They listen to his every word, they shout amen, and they put their brains to sleep. They are putty in his hands and he molds them to his will. Not only this, but they argue and bicker with others like themselves over doctrine and fight over converts. The average pagan in Africa, upon seeing eight different denominational missionaries come to his village to tell him eight different truths about the Enemy, quickly concludes that the Enemy's religion is a religion of lunatics and wants nothing to do with it.

And it is, I tell you. Why, they haven't acted like their Master for centuries. He taught poverty of spirit and world to gain eternal riches in the Enemy's palace. They all run after money and every worthless little trinket we wave at them on TV. Their Master said *"follow me"* and we have them following the almighty dollar. All well blessed, of course, by the so called Protestant work ethic, which in essence says that if you have it all in this life, you are really one of the Enemy's favorites. Elect, they call it.

He taught peace with all men, especially those of the Enemy's household. He told them to love their enemies and to do good to those who despitefully use them. But nowadays if you so much as blink the wrong way at one of them and they are ready for war. How wonderfully stupid they are! They are so easy to get angry and when they are angry, they kill people and break things while their preachers and others tell them that they are making the Enemy happy by committing war in His name. *"Blessed are the peacemakers"* HAHAHA!! They are one creation, a family united by the common blood of Adam as brothers and sisters, yet we have had them killing each other over ethnic pride and their precious little wounded egos. And if that doesn't work we fill them with lust for possessions and they go to war over land, money, possessions, etc. I love it!

But I digress. Modern Evangelicals are so lucky that they are ten generations removed from the Reformers. The Enemy doesn't even hold them guilty of rebellion any more because He says – now get this – *"they don't know any better."* In other words, He lets them off because they really don't know what they are doing by opposing the Church. They think that they are in His Church, and as long as they are baptized and keep His commandments to the best of their ability, He even forgives them for their stupid, heretical statements like *"Saved by faith alone"* which can't be found in the that Book of His. I tell you, our enemy is way too kind to them, but He says that the rules of covenant making means that their baptism entered them into the New Covenant and into the His Church, even if they don't know or acknowledge it. Therefore He can treat them not as strangers, but as the children of the covenant which even ignorant baptism makes of them.

This puts us in the odd position of attempting to get the Enemy's very own children to serve us in their ignorance. The only ones that we really have a fairly good lock upon are the pastors, after all, did not the Enemy Himself say that the more one knows, the more one is responsible. As for their parishioners, if they at least know that sin is wrong, then it is our job to get them to sin, to love it, and to leave their assembly to go live in sin. Just like that stupid Prodigal Son we managed to drive out of his household and away from his father. Ahhh, if we could only have kept him in those pig styes where he found himself after he spent all his money on that choice selection of prostitutes we provided.

That is why our Master has been so busy promoting sex without commitment. Living together. What a quaint little phrase for spitting on the Sacrament of Marriage and insulting our Enemy, Who created it. You cannot begin to know the millions of people who out of one side of their mouth swear that they know the Enemy as their friend and (ugggghhhh) Father (I despise even saying that) and out of the other side of their mouth talk about their latest live in lover. And some of them are even faithful weekly church goers! How I love that! Those liberal preachers who refuse to name such behavior as sin are some of the best captains and majors we have in our army. We may not get all their parishioners, like I said, just for the fact that they have been kept stupid by such so called preachers, but we have a veritable barbecue of these reprobate clergy going on down here and the smell of it is lovely!

This is why I told you to try get this boy of yours into fornication. He at least knows that this is wrong, so that if he falls into it, he has committed a mortal sin and loses all the grace of his baptism. Right now, because he is so ignorant of Catholic teaching, even his writings on the Internet against the Sacraments are not a mortal sin to him. Ignorance is the best defense these creatures have against the wrath of the Enemy. I'm telling you, the enemy does not fight fair. He finds every single excuse He can to forgive them, and when all fails, that Mother of His!

Oh, my hell! Her prayers for the damned drive me crazy! Just when I think I have a soul all wrapped up, one of these pestilent little insects will get the notion of praying the Rosary for that soul and asking Her to intercede for it and the next thing you know – BANG! – I lose another one. It is infuriating. I have seen more souls than I care to remember or think of be taken right out of our grasp at the very last second on the merest of technicalities and placed in that waiting room called Purgatory. We ought to sue the Enemy for breach of contract, after all, we have a thousand times as many lawyers down here as He has in His entire Kingdom, with multitudes more entering every second.

So now we have to make sure that we get these two in the end also. But something's afoot, I tell you, and I have a bad sense of this deep inside, despite my initial glee at what you did. Trouble is about now and we need to increase our vigilance to the greatest degree possible. Don't let your boy out of your sight for a second! Play him like a fine old Stradivarius violin. Don't hammer him too hard with grief and doubt of the Enemy's goodness, for he will see right through that. But you better be sure to counter every attack the Enemy places in his mind, tit for tat. If he gets some noble thought of the Enemy's "higher purposes" you be sure to wait a just a bit and then sow some real serious doubt on our Enemy's character. Be sure you make him think over and over of how <u>he</u> would have done things. We like these creatures thinking about how their plans are so much better than the Enemy's. It puffs up their ego and makes them think they are better than the Enemy, which is the first step to faithlessness and ultimately, apostasy, which is what our initial goal was for this boy. If he is made to think of how happy she is with the Enemy, you be equally sure to remind him of how empty his life seems now without her and how <u>mean</u> the Enemy was to take such a prize from him. Toss in an occasional suicidal thought. Who knows. Perhaps in a moment of rashness he will act on it and then he is ours! If he doesn't, then make him think that the Enemy is mad at him for even thinking such thoughts. That is another one of those win-win situations for us. Use guilt.

Yes, we have work to do, and plenty, but if we are vigilant, we can outplay that infernal Enemy of ours and still reap these souls. I've seen it done before, with souls more Catholic and holy than either one of these two, and it can be done again. I will be right at your side to guide you in this endeavor until we see it successfully to the end.

With gleeful but guarded celebration, I remain,

Your Uncle Infernus

CHAPTER TEN

From: darktormentum@ lake_of_fire.org

To: screamingtorture@ tormentmasters.com

Glimslug –

Nephew, I am warning you only this once! If you know what is good for you, you shall refrain from such interruptions in the future! What has gotten into you? I have been watching your work and growth with the extra assignments I have given you, and this latest episode is entirely out of character. Were you not my sister's whelp, you would be boiling in oil for the next ten years! When I am enjoying the screams of pain of some incompetent minor infernal who, through his clumsiness allowed one of these creatures to escape us and return to the Enemy, I do not like to be interrupted. And besides, your total

96

demeanor was a grave insult to my great intellect. Did you think that the plans of the Enemy and the scheming of those in His camp have somehow escaped my notice? Did I not warn you – indeed, did I not seriously warn you – that your otherwise splendid extermination of that brown haired betrayess would have repercussions somewhere down the road? And now it begins. Our Enemy makes the next move, entirely anticipated by me in my great wisdom – and you come shrieking to my door in an infantile panic! Some days I doubt I shall ever make a full fledged demon out of you.

I am not that much worried about our subject's pastor. Let him read his Bible, let him sneak off to Mass and observe it if he wishes, trying to find out why his former parishioner left his assembly and looking for some hopeful clue that she is in Heaven now. He has way too much to lose – money, job, security, and possibly wife – and besides, he will soon discover that delightful collection of abysmally dumb Catholics who couldn't theologically explain their way out of a brown paper bag if you left the top open. Once he does this, that will slow him down considerably. Just keep an eye out for that M. Jenkins and keep those two far apart. Jenkins will be respected and listened to by your pastor. The others will drive him away from the Church in frustration and confusion.

This is our stronghold over Calvinists. Because they come from a background based in Rationalism rather than faith, they refuse to believe in the mysteries of the Sacraments. They can't believe that a sacramental life of union with the Enemy is far superior to all the book learning that one could ever assimilate. Certificates lining the walls of their offices are more important than a life of prayer and charitable deeds done in the Enemy's name. And contemplative prayer? Pffffffffffffttt! Forget it! They think that scholasticism and right doctrine equals holiness! This is why the Enemy's Church, filled to the brim with dumbed down Catholics, is our biggest asset. They can't defend their faith and therefore, Calvinists are unimpressed and won't listen to them.

Yes, let him go play with the Catholics. In fact, I rather encourage it, much to your surprise. I rest assured that not only will he be appalled at the general lack of any sort of biblical knowledge among the Catholics he meets, but count on him finding and talking to one who will push him away from further investigation. You know the kind – one of those nominal Catholics who shows up to Mass out of habit and then stands outside smoking a cigarette and swearing like a truck driver. What a delightful witness to Catholicism these folks are! And they are everywhere, so I feel safe in letting him wind out his rope.

You know what else could very well happen with a little prodding from you? He could wind up Orthodox! That would be bad, but not terrible. Yes, he would be getting valid Sacraments and belong to the Enemy's ancient Church, but given his distinctly pleasant anti-Catholic nature, he would most likely become one of those Orthodox who would rather slit his wrists than to ever consider the reuniting of the Church under headship of St. Peter's Chair. I like that kind of Orthodoxy. Do you realize what would happen if the Orthodox and Catholics stopped fussing and fighting and reunited the Church? They would experience a power that would have all us demons running for the woods! Schism is such a delight. It robs the Enemy's people of any power they could have with Him. See if you can perhaps direct him to investigate that Orthodox church at the end of town. You know, the one with the priest who almost foams at the mouth every time the papacy is mentioned. We could do a lot worse than having him become that kind of Orthodox! I don't intend to lose this soul, but if things somehow get out of hand, we can minimalize the damage by having him remain anti-Catholic and anti-papal, just in a new theological framework. Who knows? He could become one of our best authors to the end of keeping the schism, anger, and mistrust between East and West going for another century or two.

Also remember that as wrong as our servants in Presbyterianism are, they nonetheless have a deep emotional sentimentality for the Enemy which they mistake for love. Therefore, if you have a bit of spare time and can direct him to a Marian Mass sometime, he will be offended right out of his socks at how they "worship" Her, and then he will sneak back to his parish, throw out all those forbidden books and that will be that. Phrases like *"Mary, Mother of God, save us who have recourse to thee."* just drive these folks crazy, and when they hear that Woman described as "Queen of Heaven and Earth" they think of the biblical injunction against worshiping the queen of heaven and they run for cover, expecting lightening to hit the bell tower at any second. They are gone like a shot, back like a jackrabbit to their little hot beds of anti-Catholicism, and we can get on with the business of damning souls since they pose no further threat to us.

If one of them actually has the nerve to ask your average Catholic why they call Mary "Mother of God" or "Queen of Heaven" they will get such a panoply of stupid and nonsensical answers that they will wander away scratching their heads in confusion. The defense of that Woman should be the easiest thing in the world for Catholics to do, yet they don't even bother trying to learn the simplest apologia. With all the good books out there written by our Enemy's lackeys, like that disgusting Scott Hahn I mentioned to you months ago, any Catholic could, in a very short time, become quite knowledgeable – and a pain in the neck to us. Ah, but they just can't turn off the TV and actually engage themselves in reading. Wonderful! We kept the world stupid and illiterate for centuries, and then when the time came that the majority of them could read, we helped the most intelligent of these vermin to invent all manner of electronic distractions so that they no longer care to read. Absolutely brilliant! Why, they must think there are going to be video games in the afterlife! Haw!!

So let him go, let him investigate, keep an eye on him, direct his movement wisely, and let us turn to the more pressing issue, that of your original subject, who has suddenly turned into a very nasty situation for us. We are in danger of no small reprimand over this one, and you do <u>not</u> want to see or experience our Dark Lord's reprimands! I know that you tried hard and many of the things you did are exactly what I would have done. I saw the way you had him on the ropes last week and to all appearances, he was just about to crumble and then out of the blue he drops to his knees and spends a whole day in fasting and prayer, crying those piteous cries that would move the heart of a stone, much less the Immaculate Heart of his Mother, who went right to that Son of Hers and obtained so much grace for Him with Her intercession that he awoke the next morning as if he were a new man.

Oh, that Woman!! She is the bane of every one of us, and sometimes, if I didn't know that our Master is going to win in the end I would be tempted to just throw it all in and quit. How ironic that he doesn't even believe that She can obtain graces for sinners and yet he is alive and well because She appeared before the Enemy's throne with those powerful prayers of Hers.

So now we are in a dilemma, and no small one at that, for he is refreshed, he trusts the Enemy again, he has decided that the Enemy can be trusted no matter what happens or where he is led, and this in turn has made him more interested than ever in studying the Enemy's Church. Hell help us if he finds out about the Traditional Latin Mass which is in the next town over. Do every thing you can to keep him from hearing anything at all about that. I know this one, I have seen this kind before, and if he gets even so much as a whiff of the Traditional

Latin Mass, we are in danger that he might even — oooooo I hate to say this but it is true — that he might even become a priest. I've seen this level of fanaticism before and the outcome is ugly to watch. We must, at all costs, keep that from happening.

He has also come to realize that wicked priests and bishops do not make the Church nor can they destroy the Church, despite our finest efforts with them and their total cooperation. Who let the cat out of the bag and informed him that they are just like the wicked priests of the Old Testament? Even when we managed to connive all of Israel into idol worship and bring it into captivity, Israel still remained in covenant with the Enemy and continued to be His peculiar people. Did someone tell him that or did he actually figure that one out on his own?

It begins to look as if we are in deep trouble with this one. We can no longer use the various and assorted wicked people of the Church against his growing interest in the Catholic Faith. He looks at every wicked priest and bishop and actually feels sorrow and compassion for them rather than hating the Church as we want him to. We have lost one of our best weapons in this fight and find ourselves at sore disadvantage. No longer will he allow his anti-Catholic friends to point out all the idiocy in the Church and use that to dissuade him from his investigation. Our Clown Masses make him sad, our liberal priests make him shake his head, our women who clamor for the right to abortion make him grind his teeth, and all he does is pray that the Enemy would remove these people from the Church and purify it.

Every day it seems that he makes a new discovery. The doctrines of the Enemy begin to make more and more sense to his logical thinking processes, the Enemy's Book suddenly reads differently, and he even tried, albeit ineptly, praying the Rosary last week!

The Rosary!

That main weapon against us! He is like a baby playing with a shotgun, but hell help us if he ever figures out how to really wield those beads! He has developed a fine case of convert fever and do I have to remind you what happens when our servants get infected with that? He will find a parish, curse us and the Master to our faces, and then proceed to turn the place upside down with his fresh faced zeal! Our only hope might be that we have one of our liberal priests in that parish, but even then, he will be a danger even to that servant of ours. I've seen converts with a case of convert fever so white hot that it literally burned all the sin out of the parish, sent the liberals packing in disgust, and taught a dozen other Catholics so deeply that three of them entered vocations in the Enemy's army! Horrible! Beyond horrible! Words fail to describe what devastation a convert can do to years and years of good solid work from a dedicated demon. It is simply not fair!

This is why I was in such a bad mood when you interrupted me. With all this and with things going from bad to worse, all I wanted was a few hours of the unrestrained pleasure of Morfglub's screams and I cannot even do that without having you barge through my door and interrupt me to tell me what I knew days ago! I have been more than aware of the situation, but there is nothing I can do right now until I further analyze the situation. His disgusting collection of apologetic books grows every week. He reads like a fiend, like a man possessed he searches out Catholic books and information. He even uses the Internet – <u>our</u> Internet full of pornography, which he should be gazing at for hours as a virile young man – to find articles written by some of the Enemy's best apologists over at Steve Ray's Catholic Convert board.

I feel sick! If I wasn't confident in my ability to come up with a plan to destroy this budding monster, I would be in absolute despair. Our infernal Master has given us a month – and I had to beg for that, reminding him of all the souls I have laid at his feet just to get that – to remedy this situation once and for all. I was going to just kill this insolent rebel once and for all, but when I went to get him, I saw the biggest guardian angel I have ever seen in my wretched existence. What is the enemy feeding those soldiers of His anyway? I've tried to kill your boy four different times, but each time the plot was foiled and he escaped. I know he is not going to join us even if I do kill him, but I am trying to do something to get the Master from going into a rage you have never in your baneful existence seen. Killing him might delight the Master, and moreover, it would most likely prevent any further collateral damage from his conversion.

Conversion? Conversion, you ask?

Heaven, yes, conversion! I am beyond a doubt that he is going to convert to the Enemy's Church. I have seen all these ugly and ominous signs before. This is – to use one of the humans' phrases – a snowball rolling downhill, and we are squarely in its path. The only thing we can do at this point is to minimize the damage. We have been doing a good job keeping him from that ex-Catholic pastor of his. That must continue. Make him afraid of the pastor. Remind him of all the ugly things that the pastor has said lately about his girlfriend's death. Keep that first anti-Catholic blow up fresh in his mind so that he wouldn't for a second consider a phone call to the pastor. We are teetering with the pastor and he could be the source of pushing him over the line. If we allow that to happen, we are in real trouble.

You know what? You can even fascinate him with the Mass if you wish, since we have already lost him to the Enemy. Going to the Mass will keep him out of his assembly and away from the possibility that he might either influence others or that pastor of his. We just cannot have anymore damage done than this. If we can minimalize the damage he does, then there is a good chance we will considerably reduce the punishment we get from the Master.

While you are at it, look for other ways to cause mischief. If you can, perhaps enlist some pimply-faced teenager into a life of homosexuality through one of those high school sexuality courses. That could be one of a number of things which might go a long way towards getting us through this. The more evil you can stir up to offset this abomination, the better it may go for us. Prove your worth as a demon and the Master may well set you free early, seeing some possible potential in you. I know you have it in you since you were so creative with that runt girl friend of his. Find one or two barflies out on a drinking binge and run their car into a van full of kids. Be creative. Just give us something to fall back on so that we get the most minimal whipping possible.

As for me, I am going to tail our boy like flies sniffing out fresh dung. If I get even a micro second where he is unprotected, I will send him to Purgatory so fast it will make your head spin! And I will be watching him all the time. A second is all I need, and we shall escape what appears to be a most unpleasant future.

Creatively in evil, I remain,

Your Uncle Infernus

CHAPTER ELEVEN

From: darktormentum@ lake_of_fire.org

To: screamingtorture@ tormentmasters.com

Unimpressive, nephew –

You come to me trembling in fear of our Master's wrath, and while little can I blame you, for he is a fearsome master of torture, I charge you now to stop cringing, act like a demon, and prepare yourself for what it is inevitably to come. I am a demon. I care not for anyone or anything, and yet you wish me to feel pity for you. That will not happen, and I must say that your cringing and whimpering before me greatly disappoints me. As the human vermin say, "Demon up!"

Face the music you have composed for yourself! What in hell is wrong with you that you would act in such a manner and express such craven cowardice? I've seen the Enemy's pets face our torturers with a steely-eyed glare which puts your behavior to absolute shame!

I will confess that it does seem unfair, for I will admit you have done an almost legendary job of work on your subject and his pastor over the last couple of months. You had everything almost under control and then in steps the Enemy and you had to watch the both of them enter the Enemy's Church on the very same day. I will give you credit for this, that even though watching that ceremony would have turned my stomach for a week, you stayed right there the whole time, and actually had the nerve to take on the guardian angels assigned to protect those apostates.

If you were trying to impress me, I thought it to be actually a rather stupid move, seeing there were two – plus several of their associates – and but one of you. I will say that you have a certain reckless lack of fear about you, and while it might strike some as bravery, I found it merely foolish and rash. Noting the beating you absorbed for your indiscretion, I would suggest that perhaps such a course of action in the future would be well worth avoiding. We absolutely despise losing our subjects to the Enemy, but you were already defeated, and they were lost for good. Nothing you could have done, even killing them before they took their vows, would have changed the outcome of their decision.

Is it really necessary for me to remind you that our enemy has a provision, called the baptism of desire, which He honors when we actually do kill one of these turncoats before they make their final vows. He sees the intent of their heart and honors that intent. When the Church was first new, we used the Jews, Romans, and various pagan tribes to kill converts as fast as they heard about and responded to that accursed Gospel. All we did was to fill the Enemy's kingdom more quickly. I don't know why, as brilliant as we demons are, it took us three hundred years to figure out this wasn't working, and to try another tactic.

All that remains now is for our Master to call us on the hot coals and tell us just how severely he shall deal with us for this complete and utter failure in guiding your subject away from the accursed Church of our Enemy. I have already emptied my office possessions into several boxes in anticipation of the coming demotion I will suffer after the Master is finished with me. I shall not only live through this, but come out even stronger than before. It is only a matter of time. When you see what the Master does to me, watch closely, and see how a real demon takes his punishment.

As for you – well, I don't know what to tell you. I would suggest that if you review all that you did in his hearing, reminding him once more of that delightful episode with Miss Simpson. Stress most strongly how well everything was going, and how good the outcome would have been, except that the Enemy once again did not play fair. Perhaps you will get lucky and he will let you off with a simple fire beating. You would do well to get your presentation well in order, making special mention of those two Episcopalian female priests you brought home to us last week. A well-presented rehearsal of all you did accomplish, accompanied perhaps by that wicked mother of yours to remind the Master of her evil charms, might possibly do some good.

Before we are summoned to answer for this, let us go over everything that transpired so that we can at least salvage something of a learning experience for you out of it all. You area demon and cannot die like humans. You will live through this, although there is the distinct possibility that you will wish and beg that you actually could die. But when you are finally over this, when you have stopped aching from the punishment you are about to endure, you must learn from this so that you can avoid such episodes in the future. It will be the wisest thing you can do in order to make the best of a wretched situation.

Of course, the first mistake you made was your inattentiveness to the mental state of your subject. Right off the bat, you should have seen that he was questioning a number of the doctrines and teachings of his Presbyterian assembly, and you should have redirected that interest into a safe area. If he was showing sacramental interest, you should have redirected him to the Episcopalians. Still in our camp, but no danger to us. That conversion would have been far less painful for the both of us. Instead, he wound up reading the Early Fathers. That twisted bunch of writings has been the downfall of a dreadful number of our faithful. Remember that, and keep your future assignments as far from those horrible preachers as you can.

You did a fairly good job of keeping him from the other converts in his town, after that lamentable start with M. Jenkins, but he did find out that the Internet has convert forums on it, and he spent way too much time in those forums and not enough in our web sites. With all great Internet apologists we have......my hell, I have a list a mile long and yet you somehow couldn't distract him into one of their sites? Nephew.....how many times am I going to have to tell you to use your resources more wisely than that! These men are absolutely brilliant in defending our heresies and they can tie up a novice like your boy for years. In fact, they can so confuse him that even as a convert, his cultural shift into thinking completely like a Catholic could have been delayed by a decade.

When a potential traitor to our cause gets to this stage, you must watch his every move, and very closely. He becomes not only a danger to himself and our plans for him, but as we saw with that pastor of his, he is a danger to many others with whom he comes into contact. It probably would have helped your cause immeasurably if your boy's parents had been Bob Jones Fundamentalists, or John MacArthur Baptists, but you can't have everything. Unfortunately for you, they are non-religious and really didn't care one way or the other about his interest in the Catholic writings he was so eagerly devouring.

Remember for the future that parents, siblings, and other family members are a rich resource. Used wisely, they can many times stop an investigation of forbidden materials dead in its tracks. The more anti-Catholic the relatives of a subject are, the more they absolutely <u>hate</u> the Enemy's Church, the better you can use them to discourage future investigations. On your next assignment, if in a thousand years you get out of the fiery pit into which you are surely to be thrown, be sure to check closely check up on the emotional and theological state of all relatives.

I will admit to a certain almost admiration at how you, a mere rookie demon, used the Enemy's Church and all the delightful apostate fools within Her to confuse and aggravate this boy. I have rarely seen such good form in constantly barraging him with weekly and sometimes almost daily doses of perverted priests, Clown Masses, inane and theologically indefensible pronouncements from clergy, cafeteria Catholics who believe only what they want to, and a host of other useful simpletons who make our Enemy's Church look like an insane asylum. The Enemy died to make His Bride the most beautiful creation on earth, a place of disgusting love and care for one another within that obnoxious sacramental worship which so pleases Him. But the Enemy made one mistake – He left the running of it to humans and they have spent two millennia peeing in the waters of their little swimming hole. It is a stunning victory for us to see just how many of these vermin humans have been turned from the Enemy simply by regarding the state of the Church He entrusted to human care!

Now – to the critical point where you actually lost this boy and caused this whole monumental tragedy:

While I admit that I got more than a little pleasure out of watching that little turncoat, Miss Simpson get her just deserts for leaving our infernal embrace, it was this one act that really cost us in souls in the long run. You cannot run off half-cocked and full of anger and just do the first thing that comes to your mind, no matter how deliciously evil it appears to you on first glance. There are repercussions for everything we do, and you have to sit down and have a long and calm talk with yourself before you act. This act of yours opened the door for every rotten thing that followed. Remember also that our Enemy does not understand what it means fight fair. By all that is just, you won that round, and should have won the whole fight from that point, yet the Enemy stepped in and twisted things so that they would produce an outcome more to His liking. Hardly cricket!

Before acting in haste, stop and ponder a minute, asking yourself: *"If this happens, will the Enemy do that? If that happens, will the Enemy then do this?"* You must be quite imaginative with this, and to that end, I suggest you embark on a long and continued study of the disgusting history of how our Enemy has used our attacks and turned them to His advantage. That Cross incident was the absolute worst of them all, but one you should think about constantly and ask yourself *"How would 'I' have done that differently?"* or, *"How could that have come out in our favor?"* Yes, we got the souls of millions who had a part in this, and who turned from their Messiah and Savior, but a very pyrrhic victory it was, for we forfeited our rulership over earth and its vermin subjects. That was the day that Paradise was opened, and they escaped our clutches in droves, beginning in Jerusalem, and then eventually throughout the whole world. Our Master was furious!

I must admit that what happened next, especially after that delicious sermon our pastor gave out, caught me completely by surprise. Out of their fondness and love for Miss Simpson, your subject and his pastor felt compelled to search for some convincing proof that perhaps Miss Simpson escaped our clutches and made it successfully to the Enemy's House. Those Calvinist rants about the elect and how *"sinners get what they deserve"* all dry up for these people when death comes to someone for whom they care. I have seen that happen in more than one Calvinist family. They tend to forget all that Jonathan Edwards *"sinners in the hands of an angry God"* blather and rhetoric, and instead start talking banally about their hopes in the Enemy's mercies for the deceased, and how perhaps their deceased loved one really was one of the elect.

I remember a Calvinist father who was quite fond of gleefully pronouncing damnation upon all the unelect of the world. But when his drunkard son died, his speech suddenly turned to his hope in the great mercy of the Enemy, even going as far as to hope aloud that his immoral son was really one of the elect. What a hypocrite! I suppose for Calvinists, it is just and right of the Enemy to damn the whole world – except for their own family members!

That was when you should have had a particular close eye on

the both of them rather than going off on a two week bender to celebrate what you thought was a rousing victory for our side. You never, underline ever assume victory in the way you did, even when all signs seem to point to what appears a complete and utter success in damnation. Danger is always just around the corner, and no more so than when we have achieved some particularly good act of evil. That pastor decided he couldn't just write off Simpson as a lost cause, a sinner getting her just deserts from a wrathful you-know-Who, so he actually went to his wife, told her how broken- hearted he was over her death, despite all the nasty things he had said that prior Sunday about her, and told her he wanted to find out if there was anything in Christian literature written anywhere, at anytime, that might offer the hope of the Enemy's mercy to her. He begged her to understand that this was not a subterfuge by which he might further investigate the Catholic Faith, but he truly wanted other input than what he had known all his Calvinist life regarding salvation and the mercy of the Enemy.

And then, his wife, completely out of left field, drops a bomb in this whole sorry episode!

"I'm so glad to hear you say that," she tells him, *"After last week's sermon, I was beginning to think you the most cold hearted person in the world. I've been wondering for a week what happened to the warm hearted man who loved people and yearned to see them be saved."*

I was sick when that conversation was reported to me by

Globscum, my newest trainee. I immediately knew right where that was heading! If only Globscum wasn't so new, if he had any idea of how to handle that situation, other than to absolutely panic, we might not be in this quandary now. You, of course, are the one who should have been there, instead of carousing around with your hot-breathed friends in a premature and unwarranted orgy of celebration. Did you somehow forget the first basic rule of damnation? You never count your souls until they are with us and well damned!

Book after book, quote after quote, author after author. And not just read in some dank little hideaway in fear for his married life – oh, no! – now our pastor brings what he considers the choicest of these quotes on the Enemy's mercies right to his wife, and she begins melting bit by bit, like an ice cube tossed in our Master's hands. Everything she heard of those old reprobates who first turned the world upside down on us made her love the Enemy even more, and further and more deeply question our lovely Calvinist doctrines which we had so carefully implanted in her mind. How could we know that she had been nursing misgivings about predestination for so long a time? How well she hid that from us! That was absolutely the ugliest of days when she said, *"You know, I have never for a second believed that God predestines babies to hell as if they are the worst of sinners and reprobates. How is that love, and the very same love that sent Christ to the Cross to die for us?"* Ugh! Very logically and well thought out question. Just the kind I hate to see forming in the minds of these insects.

Our trouble went from low to high gear in a heartbeat. He would actually sit with her at night and read aloud to her, while she looked at him with those disgusting gooey-eyed looks of love and remembered all that she had found attractive in him from the beginning. Once they reached that point, it was all over. There was no turning back his curiosity and her accompanying interest in this journey. You might – and I use that word guardedly at best – *might* have derailed their interest by introducing some of Liguouri's more flowery and intense Marian prayers into the mix, but that would have been a long shot at best. The problem with a seminary trained mind such as he has is that once they begin to examine the Greek and Hebrew, and look at overall concepts rather than some mangled literal interpretation, they will see that the Reformers played extremely fast and loose with the exegesis of Romans 3 and 4 and the fraudulent doctrine of imputed righteousness which we gave to the Reformation writers. Once that basic foundation of Calvinism crumbles, sola scriptura is not far behind to come crashing down around our heads.

Here is a word to the wise demon. If you cannot stop this ugly conversion process, which at this point is *rarely* accomplished, then try to at least draw it out and thereby delay the conversion for as long as possible. Perhaps a call from one of his old seminary buddies would have been a good thing. I once observed the rare occasion where just such a call resulted in stopping the process dead in its tracks. The potential traitor was not far along in his studies and by managing to get him to talk to the right person at the right time, we soon had him safely back in our fold, where he still resides today.

But as I said, that is a rare case indeed. The best you can hope for is to delay the betrayal for more years than is needed so that when you finally do lose your subject, he does less damage than he would have. Perhaps for the delay, he will miss converting someone who would become a major pain to us. It is better that you have him tied up puzzling over the concept of Mary as the New Eve than to be sharing his new found faith in the Enemy's Church with those shiny, bright little convert eyes.

So at this point he was lost. He found more than ample evidence of the mercy of the Enemy in the writings of the Early Fathers, and buoyed and hopeful in that, he plunged headlong into his apostasy from our ranks. At this point, instead of running around aimlessly wondering what to do next, you should have realized that your next job was to keep him from your main subject. But in such a panic you were that it never occurred to you even do that and try to minimize the damage.

And come to me, would you? Oh no! Meanwhile, the Enemy managed to steer him right into the path of your boy and once they got talking, it was like watching a fireworks factory burn from that point on. One Roman Candle of doctrine would just ignite the next with these two, and they spent hours and hours on the phone without the paying the slightest attention anymore to any of the suggestions you put in their minds, even the tried and true temptations which I personally gave you. Then, to go from bad to worse, his wife announces one night that she is convinced that the Church is the Truth, can't wait to convert, and actually presses him to enter in before Holy Saturday comes around. Three! Not one, but three souls we have lost in this dreadful mess!

Why am I not mad? Why am I not even now preparing a fine vat of oil to boil you in for a few days before we ourselves face the heat from our Dreadful Master? I honestly do not know. I have never felt this bad in all my existence and it has me, strangely enough and most fortunately for you, at a point where I just don't care. I have been sitting here staring at my favorite firewhip and thinking of all the things I could do to you with it. Yet I don't seem to be able to get up, go over to your wretched hovel, and administer another beating you so richly deserve for this massive foul up. I must be slipping.

Besides that, I think I would rather focus my efforts on seeing if there is any possible way that we can escape the most unpleasant fate, whatever our Master shall choose it to be. We have failed, and our existence from this moment on shall be marked by fear of the unknown and the surety of a most painful outcome of all this. Rage makes for unclear thinking, and right now I need some particular clarity of thought, not only to devise an escape if one is to be had, but to see if we can at least minimize the damage in some way, thus lessening the sure punishment for our dereliction of duty.

One thing that occurs to me is that now we have two men who

could still be used by us in a different manner. It is unlikely your pastor can be used, for his wife will be a steadying influence against what I am about to propose, but that boy of yours, now he still shows promising seeds of some remediation to this whole unsavory episode.

Here is what we must do: let us proceed to crank up his fledgling case of convert fever. Let us take the joy he feels over finding the true Church of our Enemy, and fan it into an <u>uncontrolled</u> white-hot flame which will make him the greatest possible annoyance to all around him. Convert fever is dangerous to us, but if carefully bent to our designs, it can be an effective tool for neutralizing damage. If used properly, we will be able to take him and drive the people in his parish into spasms of dislike for both him and Catholic orthodoxy.

There is also a fine old trick to use on coverts, and it is a shame that more demons do not press it to their advantage. Get his eyes off the Enemy and on his performance. It is easy enough to do in the heat of his conversion. I know this will sound odd, but your job now reverses. You want to make him a *very* orthodox Catholic. Encourage him. Fan these flames so that eventually he finds himself even willing to criticize things he might not like about the pope.

When he does that – you've got him!

Why?

Why, because he will suddenly have his eyes no longer fixed

upon himself as sinner, but upon his performance. As a Protestant, everything was about his performance and how much scripture he memorized. In Protestantism, it's not about how you live out the Enemy's Gospel in charity, but how you perform, therefore, everything in the Enemy's Church will suddenly have to meet the assessment of his understanding of the Catholic faith. Since he really doesn't really understand the depths of his new faith, since he will have a distinctly Protestant understanding of following the Enemy, you will be able to make a judgmental and pestilent nuisance out of him who will drive folks away from the Catholic faith instead of leading them into it.

What we most assuredly do not want is your boy teaching RCIA classes, starting parish Bible studies, encouraging the priest to run ads in the local paper, or stirring up some strange ideas of Catholic evangelism in his parish.

No, no, no!! A thousand times no!

We cannot have any of this sort of nonsense taking place in a wonderfully quiet and dead old parish. Make him a pest, a nuisance of verbal pomposity in his learning, one who drives people away from all that is orthodox because they associate it with wild-eyed fanaticism. Fanaticism is far and away our best friend now, and whenever one of these dirty turncoats leaves us, we must turn him into a fanatic so he will drive people from the Church in the same manner that garlic repels vampires. Properly done, your subject will offend the lukewarm in any parish he goes to and they will associate the Truth with him and think it something well worth left alone. Modernism is our friend, for it keeps the Enemy's children from maturing into warriors who would cause us no end of problems and most likely would empty Purgatory with their prayers. He could be a great danger to the fine modernist nonsense we have in so many of our parishes in his town, therefore, you must make a fool out of him by making him an overzealous pest who is more Catholic than the pope.

If you do your job correctly, and apply everything I have taught you about the proper placement of temptations, he will think that every carefully placed suggestion of yours which leads him into fanaticism is the Enemy speaking to him. That is just too good to watch and if he gets really crazy, you may even be rewarded with a visit from our Master to spend a day watching the fun as he offends people and then goes away thinking himself to be suffering for living a saintly and holy life. He will swear that he has the truth, that others should be listening to him, and if pushed far enough, he may even decide that the only option he has for the safety of his soul is to become an ultra radical Traditionalist or Sedevacantist of some sort. He will be written off by all as a nutcase, which he may well become in his zeal, and you could possibly obtain a nice promotion. So my advice to you is to make this your new goal once you have suffered through the Master's wrath over this dereliction of duty.

I am going away for a couple of days to think through a strategy. I would advise you to do the same. Practice the most pathetic, whimpering, groveling you know. Work on your cringing in the outright and abject fear which delights our Master so much. If you want help in this, go all the way down to Section C-1, where he spends his time taking care of miscreants like yourself. I *strongly* advise you not to be seen. Hide nearby, and after he goes in for some "personal training" of those who have disappointed him, listen carefully to the sound that comes out of that area. Filling your ears with those screams will help you develop a real cringing fear that he so likes to see, and perhaps might even help your thinking processes find a way out of this mess you have created. Perhaps you may somewhat restrain his hand.

And while you are at it, come up with a good plan to make a nutter out of our lost cause, and be ready to present it in your defense with those piteous pleas to the Master for one more chance to remedy this dreadful mess.

You will be wise if you heed what I am telling you and get busy immediately.

In the service of Hell and our Master through all, I remain,

Infernus

CONCLUSION

From: darktormentum@ lake_of_fire.org

To: screamingtorture@ tormentmasters.com

Well nephew,

It appears that this unsavory episode draws itself to a close, and to an ending which, while not what I would like, will at least keep us from enduring the dread anger of our Master. By the sheerest dint of luck, combined with preparation and the wise skill of an old demon, I have managed to have us escape a hideous fate, and also have retained my most enjoyable and envious position as a demon among demons, a master trainer of the simple, a demon to be revered among all.

How?

Why, very simple, nephew. Timing is everything! From the destroying of a soul to simplest encouragement into a life of sin – timing! I think you will agree, having learned some valuable lessons from this whole episode. Of all that you may have learned through all this, let timing be the most critical lesson you learn. A well-timed temptation is of more value than a thousand deaths. A properly timed ill witness to the Enemy's Church, such as a drunken Catholic, is of more value than a hundred liberal priests ranting and raving.

And how did I time our escape? First of all, I was aware of my surroundings. It just so happened that last week we had our annual pass in review for the year. It is a time when all the work we have done is up for review and plans are made for the coming year's warfare against souls. I had almost forgotten it in the desperate machinations of my mind to find an escape. I knew that our depraved Master would be in attendance, along with the entire infernal hierarchy, and that perhaps some positive report of evil might set the stage for me to approach him.

The second opportunity which came to me was to find myself, much to my great surprise and pleasure, to be seated in my usual place of honor (honor very befitting one so noble, brilliant, and evil as I) at the very left hand of the Master.

Think of it – at his very left hand, even after all that has come to pass with your subject. I do not know how that all came about, nor what I might have done to have found myself again there, but I knew one thing– this, my young nephew, was opportunity dropping itself right into my very lap. A most envious place to be, and one which gave me a sense that somehow I might be able to turn that seat of nearness to our Master into an advantage – if the opportunity presented itself.

And present itself it did! It came during the recitation of the year's accomplishments. Nephew, what a splendidly evil year we have had among these pathetic and disgusting vermin! Let me recite to you just the merest of statistics which were shared with us on this glorious night:

Perhaps our greatest single area of success is our pornography enterprise, which has grown exponentially over the last year. We have a 17% increase in addictions by married men and an 8% increase in the clergy. That is an astounding success by any measure. When this figure was read, I quickly glanced to my right, and saw just the slightest of movement from the Master. The figures touched something within him, and while no expression crossed his face, it was not hard to see that he liked what he was hearing. In addition to this, we have seen an increase in the use of all kinds of contraceptive devices. These pathetic creatures use each other's bodies like so much toilet paper, having not the least regard for each other as made in the image of God and worthy of being treated with respect. Of course, such disrespect leads them to treat the products of their fornication as things rather than beings, and they continue to butcher their unborn in staggering numbers.

Such bloody fun! A day spent in possession of the body of some abortionist doctor on his murderous rounds is one of the most refreshing vacations any demon can treat himself to. Not only does that demon get to participate in that doctor's damning of his own soul, but he gets to vicariously rip apart the emerging life, and ruin the life of the woman. That is just too good. I happen to know that from time to time our infernal Master actually participates in such possession. This all came from our great friend, Hugh Hefner, when he got us started in this enterprise some forty years ago. All this deviance is must continue into each new generation, therefore, it is very important that the pornography enterprise continue to be carefully cultivated for the fine work of damnation it is doing in the world. What a great cursing it is!

The Enemy's Church has lost another 14% to our various heretical denominations and sects. In addition, several new religions have formed, all of which have precious little to do with the Enemy other than using the generic word for Him — the one that starts with "G". On top of that, the Enemy's agents on earth don't appear to have the foggiest clue as to how to respond to this attack, and we are emptying the Church at an ever increasing pace. Again, I noticed a shift of position in his throne as our infernal Master allowed all this to sink in. He seemed to take particular delight in hearing that there are three new self-proclaimed messiahs roaming the world, deluding ever-increasing numbers of followers as they claim to be the incarnation of the Enemy. That is just too rich an insult for our Master not to like.

We also made great gains in the political arena as country after country elected warmongers, abortionists, and especially those in favor of gay "marriage." Laws are already pending in several countries which will make these delightful perversions of real marriage completely legal. The Enemy's troops are in complete disarray as they face this. They are so unlike that bunch of apostates of the first century, who by a single word could strike down our people. Why, the enemy doesn't even have any real prayer warriors anymore. There was a time that the Enemy's troops knew how to fast and pray, and I'm telling you, we lost more than a few of our finest troops to the smiting hand of angels turned loose in vengeance by those prayers.

Remember those thirty Roman procreates of the second century who were persecuting the Church, and what happened to them as a result of the prayers of the Enemy's persecuted people ? That was truly horrible! Good for us, of course, because we reaped their souls, but we had such plans for them and suddenly – BANG – one by one they were picked off by those prayers within the span of a mere month. I shudder to think what will happen if the Enemy's troops ever relearn such an ability to pray.

Speaking of prayers, fewer and fewer of the Enemy's people are praying that dreaded Rosary anymore. This is exceedingly good news. We have all but the very best of them so busy chasing after foolishness and the possessions of life that they come home exhausted, watch TV, and fall asleep in their comfy little chairs. Some warriors they are! I tell you, I wouldn't be afraid of a thousand of them if they were each a hundred feet tall. A weaponless soldier is my favorite enemy, and our

Enemy's soldiers have put down their prayer weapons and surrendered without so much as a whimper. Fewer Rosaries, fewer of the Chaplet of Divine Mercy, therefore much less power, and less aggravation to our plans.

Do you want to know why? Because we are making converts in some places at a staggering rate! Why, almost all of Brazil has left the Enemy's camp, and those who are left are nominal and ineffective at best. Of course, on their way out the doors, they tear their Rosaries into pieces, destroy their Scapulars, and throw away any dusty prayer books they have lying around in a corner. Not that they were much of warriors for the Enemy anyway. It is refreshing to see how easily they are taken in by our troops and the lies we have given them to promote.

After those good reports there were the more usual yearly reports which came in without any particular excitement. You know, the usual newly consecrated bishops who don't believe a bit of it, more Protestant clergy molesting children and beating their wives, new translations (or should I say mistranslations) of that Book the Enemy left for them, the usual greed, production of more new toys to encourage them in that greed and keep their minds from pursuing the Enemy. Yack, yack, yack. All pretty much boring. I was still hoping for a chance, just an opening, but things at this point were beginning to look like they were going from bad to worse as far as my seizing an opportune moment.

And then it happened – that instant of perfect timing that I knew

I could use to my advantage. Such a wonderful and damnable report, for it brought the Master to his feet in applause, and for the first time that day, I saw a bit of a sardonic smile cross his face. Yes, this was the crowning moment, when Mugvomus turned in his report on the newest and potentially brightest area of insult and attack upon the character of the Enemy– human/animal crossbreeding!

Imagine that! It is not enough that we have these pathetic creatures crawling around in the most depraved sins acting like animals, murdering their own infants before they are even born, fornicating each other into deadly diseases with a ferocity unheard of. Now we are going to get them to cross breed themselves with animals and mar the image of God in them permanently! Their scientists came up with this, and Mugvomus has brought it home to completion. It is amazing how the evil mankind comes up with by themselves can make us look absolutely infantile in comparison.

Chimeras! Glorious!

When this was announced, our Master – now think of this – actually stood to his feet and applauded the work of this noble degenerate demon. To think that we have actually managed to drag man so far down in his view of life and himself that he would mix the genes of man and animal and come up with a hybrid that is neither. Brilliant!

It was that very moment that I saw my opportunity. It was now or never, for never again might I find the Master in such a mood to hear the bad news I had been carrying in my breast for day after fearful day.

"Oh, Most Glorious and Brilliant Infernal Master, Darkness of Darkness" I addressed him, touching the hem of his garment ever so lightly *"When this is all over, and we have drunk deeply of the pleasures of this most vile and evil moment, might I have the shortest of words with you?"* I thought my voice was perfectly filled with fawning and fear, enough that perhaps he would grant me the audience I desired so that I could grovel at his feet.

When he turned I thought I saw the curling lines of an ironic smile creep across his face.

"You lost them, didn't you?" he said, with that knowing look that comes from centuries of dealing with the gains and losses of damnation of souls. There is precious little in the Underworld of which he is not aware at all times.

"Yes, Master. Despite our best efforts and all..."

"Enough. This is a glorious day of tremendous and delicious evil. Do not trouble yourself anymore about it. There shall be no retribution. This is a night of celebration and orgy. It is not the first soul I have lost and will not be the last, but tonight....tonight we celebrate the coming of a degradation upon those misfit humans that will bring rivers of insult to my Enemy for centuries to come."

So we are free, nephew. It is passed over, thanks to the glorious efforts of Mugvomus, and my immaculate sense of timing. Remember well this lesson, for it may well save your hide somewhere in the future when our Enemy thwarts your plans and lays waste to your best efforts. You can count upon it, so be a very wise demon and have yourself always on alert.

In the meantime, I shall shortly have a new assignment for you, in addition to your required oversight and cultivation of fanaticism into your newly lost subject. I expect to see a much better effort from you now, given all that you should have learned from this profoundly distasteful episode. I know it will feel odd at first, but you are now to turn your subject into an extreme Catholic fundamentalist, a walking, talking, and most annoying defender of the Council of Trent, and all that took place between Trent and Vatican II. With the proper oversight from you, guiding him ever so skillfully in to the fanaticism to which these converts are quite prone, you will be able to nullify him as a threat to our plans for others.

More than that, rumor has it that we are on the verge of something very delightful which I have seen before, and it bodes well for our work of dragging of souls into eternal torment. Good and well founded sources have it that the Enemy's extreme and great patience has reached the breaking point with this latest biological insult by His creatures. He is extremely close to bringing justice to bear upon these miserable wretches for their insistent evil ways, their dedication to our Master's principles, and the rivers of innocent blood they have spilled in war and abortion. If what I have heard is verifiable, they have no idea the horror which is coming their way!

Mark my words well, I have seen the Enemy execute justice on His creatures a couple of times before, and not only is it tremendously gratifying to see Him smite those pestilent little beasts left and right, but it will fill hell as you cannot even begin to imagine. It is a strange and fearful thing to be a human, for our Enemy gives them freedom of will and choice so that they can be indeed in His very image, but He holds them accountable for all that they do, and that is the fearful part.

He has done everything He can do to guide them, first by the sending of prophets by which He told them He was coming to visit them. At our bidding, they killed the prophets and eventually brought a wonderful doom upon themselves by which they were overrun by their enemies, brought in to captivity, and subjected to the vilest of torments. It took them centuries to repent and get the Enemy to release them from His chastening hand. How delightful that was!

Even better than that was watching how these ungrateful vermin treated Him when He actually came to live among them. He simply poured out His love upon them, healing all their sick, releasing them from our bondage, even raising the dead – it was so disgusting to have to watch – and what does He get for it — they crucify Him!!

I only regret how in that delicious episode of suffering the Enemy completely blind-sided us. He took His own death and turned it into the greatest defeat we have known up to this point in our noble warfare against His oppressive rulership. We were not ready for that!

How dare He apply that death to the sin of Adam so that the whole human race could be freed from our clutches? Before that we had them all, and none – not a single one, I tell you – would have ever made it to the Enemy's palace. Now they are all freed, we can no longer hold them, and we have the hard work of rounding up all these stray beasts one by one, as many as we can deceive into following our Master's evil way.

It has not been a work without certain delights, and surely we have collected an immensely large group to join us down here, but if only we had known and refrained from inciting that mob, we could have had them all forever! The only good thing of this is how utterly blind these creatures continue to be. They are so filled with every wonderful hatred that they kill the Enemy's missionaries, they destroy the Enemy's churches, and they burn that Book when they can get their hands on it. They are marvelously blind to the fact that the Enemy is trying to keep them from being with us forever. And through all this, the Enemy just keeps sending out more of His soldiers to speak to them.

Finally, in closing, I share with you one last fable which goes back to ancient times, a story which, I remind you, that if true, means that we must be always busy and always about our Master's business. It has commonly been noised about here for centuries that one day the Enemy is planning to return to live among them as their King. Supposedly He is going to raise the dust that used to be their bodies and reconstruct them so that they can live with Him forever. I also hear such of this story that the Enemy will cast us out of His Church, sending all our double agents down to us, and will bind us forever to keep us from those creatures He loves. This story gives the infernal bipedal pests no small amount of deluded comfort, since they think the Enemy, to whom they are enslaved, is going to somehow take over what rightfully belongs to our Dark Master.

Well, we shall see about that. The Master has assured me that unlike the first visit to Earth which the Enemy made, he will be ready. One day when this fable came up, the Master told me that he has thought and rethought upon every possible contingency, and when the Enemy comes – well, if it's war He wants, it will be war He gets! I have every confidence in our Dark Master, therefore, while we have time left unfettered by this coming glorious conflict, left us go forth to damage the Enemy as much as we can, and reap as many souls as possible for the dark glory of our evil Master. When the war comes, we will no longer be able to reap souls and enjoy watching their torment, knowing that it was by our efforts that they suffer eternally. We shall be busy defeating the Enemy for our Dark Master, and damning humans shall have to be temporarily put aside.

I have a fine vintage bottle of Old Fireball that I have been saving for a very special occasion. Escaping as we did our Dark Master's wrath has every appearance to me of being that occasion, therefore, I have uncorked said bottle, and am in the process of draining it. Do not bother coming over. I shall be quite incommunicado by this evening, and anyway, you are not company I care to keep – even when I am drunk. You, nephew, are one very lucky little demon that you were under my tutelage when you made these thoughtless blunders, or you would be screaming in pain now. So go celebrate for a few days a freedom you do not deserve and pain you are not suffering. When you return we shall once again be busy as I hone you into the finest of warriors for our dreaded Master. After all, am I not...

The greatest, smartest, and best trainer in hell,

Infernus the Magnificent

TRAINER'S REPORT

From: darktormentum@ lake_of_fire.org

To: Most_High_Dark_Lord@ Imperial_Throne.org

To His Most Glorious Darkness, Lord of the Underworld, Rightful Lord of all Creation, Incomparable in Wisdom, All Wise Potentate, He From Whom We All Get our Substance, to Whom I Bow in Groveling Respect and Fear:

It is with the greatest pleasure that I respond to your commands, now and always your loyal servant, until you bring an end to all things. As per your request, I now submit for your approval the requested review of my most recent trainee, one Glimslug of note. Hoping that this review will meet not only with your approval, but with a resultant increase in my duties in your most glorious service, offer you the following information regarding this, your subject, Glimslug.

As you know, the subject does have relation to me, however, I in no way have allowed this to color the objectivity of this report. Rather, being most painfully aware of certain failures on the part of this subject, I have worked quite carefully to present an objective report of this subject's work in his initial training period. It is hoped that you shall find all in order and much to your liking.

Glimslug is a fine specimen of evil, having apparently had the good fortune of being whelped by two insidious demons who are not lacking in any pursuit of evil. We can be thankful that the majority of those flesh bags called humans are not in any way as dedicated to the principles of their Master, our Enemy, as these two demons are to following the standards of your most glorious and evil rule. As a result, when the subject was presented to me, he was a fine specimen of surliness, mouthiness, arrogance, insolence, and general evil, which I felt immediately upon our meeting that I could mold into a great warrior in the battle for the damnation of souls. He has not disappointed.

Glimslug appears to be a most wise demon, for once in my presence, and having given to him a small dose of the pain which could be his for a considerable time if he decided to pursue his reckless abandon in my presence, he quickly settled into a compliant and teachable state, understanding fully his place in this hierarchy. But make no mistake, under that guise of subordination I am still quite able to see that once he is promoted, he will become every bit as overbearing and arrogant as the best of those who are now his masters. I do not exaggerate to state that I believe that one day this outstanding specimen will present himself as my equal in all traits and characteristics of evil. It will only be with the greatest effort that I will keep him from overthrowing my position and assuming all the rights and perks I have so long and hard worked for.

Rest assured, however, in the knowledge that this simply shall not happen, for one does not attain to the great age I have, nor the long practice of evil, without developing several tricks of which he knows nothing. It will be wisdom on his part if he attains equality with me without challenging me for my position. Believe me when I say that having observed the quality of his work, I have become oddly fond of him and would find it distasteful to administer tutorial pain to him on any level. Do not, my Master, in any way regard that last statement on my part as an indication of any weakness or lack of ability to deal severely with him – or anyone for that matter – who would challenge me. I simply state that I appreciate the finer qualities of his insolent and evil bearing among the demonic underworld.

Regarding the aforesaid quality of his work, let us now turn to the review of his work which you have requested:

During the most recent shortage of demonic powers, Glimslug was assigned a most difficult task for a novice, that of keeping a potential convert to our Enemy's Church from making that actual defection, and thus becoming a warrior against our cause. It goes without saying that the more intelligent these human vermin are, the worse they are to deal with when they actually begin to think of converting to the Enemy's camp. The very mind which we use to come up with a thousand strange and esoteric excuses for not believing in the Enemy's doctrines, nor joining the Enemy's Church, suddenly becomes our worst enemy. With the unfair addition of just a touch of grace from the Enemy, the thought process of the potential convert is suddenly turned against us, and we are bombarded almost continually with one situation after another which we have to bring under control. For a master of darkness, this is challenge enough, but for a novice, this is an extremely difficult situation, almost to the point of being unfair. Yet it is understandable that you, in your great wisdom, knew that this situation could not be allowed to continue unchecked. Therefore, despite his raw novice condition, the gravity of the situation demanded that he be "thrown into the fire" as it were.

Indeed it proved to be a real baptism of fire for our trainee, yet he rose to the challenge on more than one occasion. Allow me remind you of some of the more memorable occasions of fledgling success which he enjoyed:

During the first few months, Glimslug learned well how to confuse a subject by using the subject's fear of damnation against him It is not without reason that we had those wonderful subjects of ours, the Reformers, clamoring that membership in the Enemy's Church is a sure ticket to a front row seat in hell. Not only did they use such fear to drag converts out of our Enemy's Church, but they created literature of such volume that centuries of mankind have been deceived and kept from converting. The most hideously laughable part of that is that out of fear of losing their souls, they ran away from the very Institution which our Enemy placed on earth for the salvation of their miserable souls. Many of them now reside in the deepest torments of your most glorious leadership.

My dark and fearful Master, is that not just deliciously ironic?

When the enemy responded unfairly by touching the Enemy's pastor with a little bit of grace, Glimslug responded just as I instructed him. While not losing any of his arrogance, his hatred for these miserable vermin, a beautiful thing to behold in so young a demon, made him the most pliable and teachable of subjects. While I could see that some days he was almost biting his tongue to keep from being insubordinate, his hatred made him so want to destroy any and all of your enemies that he listened and applied himself with a vigor I have rarely seen in my many years of training novices.

May I also remind you of his creativity in doing evil? When his subject was being overwhelmed with poisonous lies by a young female who had recently escaped our clutches, Glimslug took a course of action which has resulted in several souls being led directly into our camp. Not only did I have the distinct pleasure of watching the young female turncoat be smashed into a bloody pulp by a drunken truck driver, but the driver, in a fit of remorse, put a gun to his head a week later, and dispatched himself directly into your waiting arms. The resultant lawsuit against the driver's company bankrupted the company some six months later, and caused the owner to turn to alcohol and adultery to ease the pain of his loss. I have no doubt that we shall inevitably reap his soul also.

In addition to that, three of the families who belonged to the turncoat's assembly have so stiffened their souls against the Enemy's Church that conversion for them would be a greater miracle than raising the dead. One even brought her parents into the assembly and after a day of pleading with them to save their souls, got them to forsake the Enemy's Church. It was such a pleasure to watch her plead with them for hours, begging them to get saved. She was convinced by a stirring sermon preached by her pastor that her parents would suffer the same fate at the hands of the Enemy, and would not leave until they made a decision for ......well, you-know-Who.

One of the most satisfying days of my life came when those parents made vows to enter that Presbyterian denomination in their town and verbally spit upon and disowned the Enemy's Church. Being that they arc well advanced in age, we shall soon have them in our grasp for their insolent turning against the only source of salvation with such a reckless abandon. How sad for them that if they had paid as much attention to the teachings of the Enemy's Church as they did to that worthless TV they wasted hours in front of, they would have spared themselves an eternity of suffering for their mindless insolence against the Enemy. But how good for us. There is simply nothing finer for our cause then the laziness and self-indulgence of those who profess to love the Enemy.

Speaking of that pastor, while the Enemy did play foul and gave him a touch of grace, enough that for some strange reason, he defected from our noble cause, Glimslug followed my orders explicitly and remedied the situation. What could have been a disaster for us turned into a most satisfying quasi-victory. While we would have desired nothing less than the continuous fidelity of this pastor to your glorious cause, Glimslug has negated any good that he might have done in the Enemy's cause. Indeed, having responded to the initial touch of grace which made him sympathetic to the Enemy's cause, he has been carefully manipulated into a hyper-critical fundamentalist Catholic of the worst sort regarding the condition of the Enemy's Church. He has become a pariah in his family, who at first regarded his return to the Enemy's Church with joy. They now regard him as a full blown nutcase and go to every means to keep him from visiting them. Tact is always somewhat lacking in converts, and Glimslug has well used this to our advantage with this turncoat's family. Even as I type, Glimslug continues to most carefully work this man into a more complete agent of discord within the Church. He has taken this traitor's love for the Enemy and is using it directly against him. I would not be surprised to see him become a Sedevacantist somewhere down the road. He is thoroughly and completely neutralized.

My most exalted Master, that is bringing victory out of the ashes of defeat, and to watch Glimslug work on this traitor, one would have thought he had been doing this kind of work for a thousand years. He is indeed an excellent student of the damning arts. We may have lost the souls of this pastor and his wife, but the creation of him as an opponent of the Enemy's Church, and the destruction he will cause for the next many years, will be lovely to behold.

While it is true that there was a momentary dereliction of duty in which Glimslug went on a premature drunken binge of celebration, upon his return, and after my painful reprimand, he rededicated himself to the damning arts. From that time forward, Glimslug did not take the usual vacations for rest and reflection upon the art of damnation that most novice demons are accustomed to taking. No, your Infernal Majesty, his hatred for mankind has matured to such a degree of malice that he wishes he never had to rest in the pursuit of their damnation. As this hatred grew, he pursued many small side projects which I allowed him for training purposes, with the following admirable results:

1. The damnation of two Episcopalian priestesses who were considering the recanting of your most glorious doctrines to join the

Enemy's Church. This was a most salutary piece of work because these two women were first delicately returned to a state of enmity to the Church. *"That ancient institution run by out of touch old white men,"* as they so beautifully put it. Then, when Glimslug had determined that there was not even the hint of anything resembling a baptism of desire for the Enemy's Church, he proceeded to get them rip-snorting drunk and drive them in front of a train.

My, that was glorious to behold! Glimslug was right there, too, grabbing their souls from their bodies and waving them about in triumph like an Olympian waving about his country's flag. My Master, I think you shall grow to appreciate this young demon, his hatred for souls, and his dedication to your cause. He is absolutely filled with the vilest hatred for humans and with even the slightest shred of pity towards them, not even to the point of giving the damned a quick and painless death on their way to Hell. No, my Master, the more pain he can inflict upon them, the better he likes it.

2. The removal of two priests from the diocese in which they worked. This was a savagely beautiful piece of work. Glimslug managed to convince the local authorities, through the use of "recollected memories" in two teenagers, that these priests had supposedly molested these young men as children. Of course, nothing of the sort had happened, but with the current hysteria which has overtaken the Church, it was a fine piece of deception to convince the authorities that indeed such an occurrence did happen. Going from person to person, and from mind to mind (if these creatures could be said to possess minds), he stirred the community into a bubbling caldron of outrage. Reason gave way to howls of outrage and calls for justice. Never mind that there was not a shred of evidence set before anyone in this matter. With human beings, all you must do to stir up trouble is work on their emotions. The rest is fairly easy once you get that caldron boiling.

The end result of this work is that these two priests, who were orthodox troublemakers of the worst sort, are gone. And by gone, I do not mean that they simply were transferred to another diocese. Oh, no! They are gone for good. The one has recanted his priesthood and returned to the secular life and wants nothing to do with the Enemy's Church at all (who could blame him, being so unjustly handled) and the other one, while a still a priest, is broken and quiet. The ministry he had to children, which was his gift from the Enemy, has been terminated in him for good. He dares not go near children and parents in the town want nothing to do with him. Furthermore, this smear, even having proven untrue, will dog him the rest of his rotten life. We have won a great victory here, and Glimslug has done so. The parish is now led by two liberals who, while not exactly on our side, are not troublemakers either. The one is lazy, lacking the devout life that priests should have, and the other one, while more orthodox, has the personality of a porcupine. People don't even like going to Confession with him. The

146

parish is on the verge of internal schism, the people have gone from enthused to bored, and many families have simply left. Making trouble like this is not just good for our cause, it provides a fine level of entertainment as well.

3. As Glimslug worked with his first subject, he rapidly developed formidable skills in deceit. In his time away from his subject, he asked to be assigned to another potential convert – and absolutely turned this one around! I found myself amazed at the delicate touch that Glimslug had developed over a period of time under my tutelage. The skills I saw him manifest usually take three to four times as long to master as they did in him. Indeed, I could only marvel at the way he directed this potential convert to find all of our reading material against the Church and filled this one's mind with lies and drivel about the Enemy's Church. It was not even necessary to use the fear of damnation on this particular potential turncoat. We have such a fine library of books as resources for our demons to use. I am amazed that this new subject, who greatly enjoys reading, had never seen Lorraine Boettner's lying little wonder called ROMAN CATHOLICISM. That book is one of the finest pieces of authorship we have out there, and it is well known to most dedicated Protestants, yet Glimslug's new subject was entirely unfamiliar with it. He followed up that initial offering with the usual brilliance of Jack Chick and James White and in no time had is subject safely back into his Lutheran assembly where to this day he thinks he is serving the Enemy and pleasing Him. If I were grading that action alone I would have given Glimslug a pure and perfect 10. It was a marvelous effort, and worthy of one who has been trained by the best demon trainer in Hell.

Our final count for this training session is as follows:

7 souls delivered directly into hell

3 souls stiffened like iron against the Enemy's Church

2 souls as defectors creating chaos in the Enemy's Church.

2 priests disposed of

1 potential convert turned from the enemy's Church and

1 parish on the verge of anarchy and collapse.

I think you would agree with me that by any standard, this has been a most glorious and well done training. It is therefore without reservation that I not only present with pride this report to your most Infernal Majesty, but strongly suggest that this young demon be promoted to Darkness First Level with all according honors. I do not expect it too take too long for his continued work to be noticed by the ranks of hell. He has already taken on a rather large project involving a school district and the so called rights of homosexuals to teach their behavior as normal, and the project is showing every sign of bearing much fruit in future perversions and the filling of hell with more souls.

I have no doubt that upon the successful conclusion of this project you will want to promote him to Darkness Second Level and make the award yourself.

It has been a rare pleasure to work with a demon so dedicated to the destruction of souls, and for this, I humbly grovel at your feet in thanks for this privilege.

With humblest groveling before your most Dark Majesty, I remain,

Your loyal servant, Infernus

Darkness General Three

.

www.ingramcontent.com/pod-product-compliance
Lightning Source LLC
Chambersburg PA
CBHW071001040426
42443CB00007B/605